CROWN FINANCIAL MINISTRIES

BIBLICAL FINANCIAL STUDY

COLLEGIATE EDITION

STUDENT MANUAL

ISBN 10-digit: 1-893946-11-8
ISBN 13-digit: 978-1-893946-11-8

May 2003 Edition

HOMEWORK AND PRACTICAL APPLICATION SCHEDULE

Week	Homework	Practical Application
1	Introduction	Personal Information Sheet
2	God's Part	Personal Financial Statement / Recording Income & Spending
3	Our Part	Deed / Career and Financial Goals
4	Work	Resumé / Job Interview
5	Debt	Debt List
6	Honesty	Estimated Budget
7	Counsel	Adjusting Your Budget
8	Giving	Beginning Your Budget
9	Investing	Insurance / Investing
10	Your Future	Checking Account / Budget Summary

REQUIREMENTS

This study is designed to be taught in either a college class or a small group setting. Everyone must complete these requirements before each weekly class:

1. HOMEWORK

Complete the homework in writing. The homework questions are designed to take approximately fifteen minutes each day to complete. Space is provided in the study manual to answer the homework questions.

2. SCRIPTURE MEMORY

Memorize an assigned verse each week.

3. PRACTICAL APPLICATION

Each week complete a practical exercise, such as beginning a budget or formulating a debt repayment schedule.

If you are taking this study in a small group:

1. Everyone prays for their group members each day.
2. If for any reason someone does not complete all the requirements for a particular week, the teacher or small group leader is not to allow them to participate in the discussion that week. This accountability cultivates faithfulness; the more faithful a person is, the more benefits he or she will derive from the study.

If you are taking this study for credit, your professor will assign additional work.

PURPOSE

The purpose of the CROWN FINANCIAL MINISTRIES study is to teach people God's financial principles in order to know Christ more intimately and to be free to serve Him.

FINANCIAL POLICY

CROWN FINANCIAL MINISTRIES does not endorse, recommend or sell any financial products or services or give specific investment advice. No one may use their affiliation with CROWN FINANCIAL MINISTRIES to promote or influence the sale of any financial products or services or give investment advice.

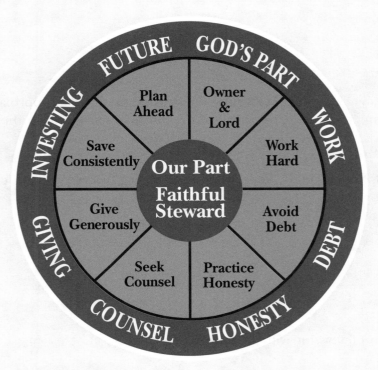

How We Handle Money Impacts Our Fellowship with the Lord—

"If therefore you have not been faithful in the use of worldly wealth, who will entrust the true riches to you?"

LUKE 16:11

MEMORIZE
LUKE 16:11
"If therefore you have not been faithful in the use of worldly wealth, who will entrust the true riches to you?"

Memorize Luke 16:11 and complete the homework on the next page prior to attending the first class.

Read Isaiah 55:8-9.

Based on this passage, do you think God's financial principles differ from the way most people handle money? What do you think is the greatest difference?

Then read Luke 16:11.

What does this verse communicate to you about the importance of managing possessions faithfully?

How does handling money impact our fellowship with the Lord?

 My prayer request for the coming week:

Scripture memory hints and principles: Read several verses before and after the memory verse to gain an understanding of its context in the Bible. Learn and repeat the reference each time you review the verse. Break the passages into natural phrases and learn one phrase at a time. The memory verses are found on page 3 of the Practical Application Workbook and may be removed and carried with you throughout the day.

* The words *worldly wealth* from the New International Version have been substituted for the words unrighteous mammon from the New American
  Standard Version to clarify the meaning of Luke 16:11.

INTRODUCTION NOTES

Two economic systems operate in the world, God's economy and the economy that people devise. Scripture reveals God's economy to us in great detail.

The way most people handle money is in sharp contrast to God's financial principles. This should not surprise us. Isaiah 55:8 reads, *"For My thoughts are not your thoughts, neither are your ways My ways,' declares the Lord."* The most significant difference between these economic systems is that in God's economy the living Lord plays the dominant role. This distinction has profound practical implications.

Most people view God's economy as being based upon an irrational "leap of faith." Because God has chosen to be invisible and operates in the unseen, supernatural realm, God's economy appears to have no logical foundation. The person who does not yet know the Lord has a hard time comprehending God's economy. Paul wrote in his first letter to the Corinthians,

> *But a natural man does not accept the things of the Spirit of God; for they are foolishness to him, and he cannot understand them, because they are spiritually appraised. But he who is spiritual appraises all things.*
>
> 1 CORINTHIANS 2:14-15

THE BIBLE AND MONEY

It surprised me to learn just how much the Bible says about finances. There are approximately 500 verses on prayer, fewer than 500 on faith, but more than 2,350 verses on how to handle money. We need to ask ourselves why Jesus Christ Himself said more about it than almost any other subject. He lived in a much simpler society than ours, He never had to deal with the temptations of a credit card, and I suspect He never even had to reconcile His checkbook!

There are at least three reasons why money and material possessions were a constant theme in His teaching.

There are approximately 500 verses on prayer, fewer than 500 on faith, but more than 2,350 verses on how to handle money.

1. How we handle our money impacts our fellowship with the Lord. Jesus equates how we handle our money with the quality of our spiritual life. In Luke 16:11 we read, *"If therefore you have not been faithful in the use of worldly wealth,* who will entrust the true riches to you?"* If we handle our money properly according to the principles of Scripture, our fellowship with Christ is going to grow closer. If we are unfaithful with it, our fellowship with Him will suffer.

This is clearly illustrated in the parable of the talents. The master commends the servant who had managed money faithfully: *"Well done, good and faithful slave; you were faithful with a few things; I will put you in charge of many things. Enter into the joy of your master"* (Matthew 25:21). Scripture is very clear; those who faithfully handle money have the opportunity to enter into the joy of a more intimate relationship with our Lord. Sadly, this is a fundamental biblical truth which most people have failed to grasp.

2. Possessions compete with the Lord for mastery of our lives. That is why Jesus had so much to say about money. He tells us we must choose to serve only one of these two masters.

> *No one can serve two masters; for either he will hate the one and love the other, or he will hold to one and despise the other. You cannot serve God and mammon [money].*
>
> MATTHEW 6:24

It is impossible for us to serve money—even in a small way—and still serve the Lord.

When the Crusades were being fought during the 12th century, the Crusaders purchased the services of mercenaries to fight in their behalf. Because it was a "religious" war, the Crusaders insisted that the mercenaries be baptized before fighting. As they were being baptized, the mercenaries would take their swords and hold them out of the water to symbolize that Jesus Christ was not in control of their swords. They had the freedom to use their weapons in any way they wished.

Though not as blatant about it as were the mercenaries, many people today handle their money in a similar fashion. Some Christians hold their wallets or purses "out of the water," in effect saying, "God, You can be the Lord of my entire life except in the area of money—that is my right, and I am perfectly capable of handling it myself."

3. Much of life revolves around the use of money. The Lord talked so much about money because He also knew that much of our lives would revolve around its use. Fortunately, He has adequately prepared us for that task by giving us the Bible as His blueprint for living.

> *T*he Lord talked so much about money because He knew that much of our lives would revolve around its use.

8

A DIVISION OF FINANCIAL RESPONSIBILITIES

A close friend, Jim Seneff, challenged me to join him in a study of Scripture to find out exactly what the Lord said about handling money. We read the entire Bible, identified each of the 2,350 verses, then arranged them by categories according to their various topics. Not only were we astounded at how practical the Word of God is in this area, but we discovered there is a division of responsibilities in the handling of our money. Simply put: God has a part, and we have a part!

God has retained certain responsibilities and has delegated other responsibilities to us. Most of the frustration we experience in handling money is because we do not realize which responsibilities are ours and which are not. However, when we learn God's part and then discharge our part faithfully, we can experience contentment.

LEARNING TO BE CONTENT

Contentment is mentioned seven times in the entire Bible, and six times it has to do with money. One of our goals during this study will be that you will learn to become financially content. In Philippians 4:11-12, Paul writes, *"For I have learned to be content in whatever circumstances I am. I know how to get along with humble means, and I also know how to live in prosperity."*

Examine these verses carefully. We are not born with the instinct of contentment; rather, it is something we must learn.

Next week's homework assignment will address God's part. Let me caution you that as you complete this homework, it may seem as if God does everything. However, we are not to adopt a passive or fatalistic attitude. The Lord has given us specific authority and responsibilities to fulfill. We will be studying our various responsibilities for eight full weeks!

When we learn God's part and then discharge our part faithfully, we can experience contentment.

The Lord Is Owner of All—

"Everything in the heavens and earth is yours, O Lord . . ."

1 CHRONICLES 29:11, LB

**MEMORIZE
1 CHRONICLES
29:11-12, LB**
"Everything in the heavens and earth is yours, O Lord, and this is your kingdom. We adore you as being in control of everything. Riches and honor come from you alone, and you are the Ruler of all mankind; your hand controls power and might, and it is at your discretion that men are made great and given strength."

**PRACTICAL
APPLICATION**
Complete the Personal Financial Statement and begin keeping a record of everything you spend.

DAY ONE _____

Read Deuteronomy 10:14; Psalm 24:1 and 1 Corinthians 10:26.

What do these passages teach about the ownership of your possessions?

Then read Leviticus 25:23; Psalm 50:10-12 and Haggai 2:8.

List the specific items in these verses that the Lord owns?

Leviticus 25:23 —

Psalm 50:10-12 —

Haggai 2:8 —

Prayerfully evaluate your attitude of ownership toward your possessions. Do you consistently recognize the true owner of those possessions? Give two practical suggestions to help recognize God's ownership.

1.

2.

DAY TWO _____

Read 1 Chronicles 29:11-12 and Psalm 135:6.

What do these verses say about the Lord's control of circumstances?

Then read Proverbs 21:1; Isaiah 40:21-24 and Acts 17:26.

What do these passages tell you about the Lord's control of people?

Proverbs 21:1—

Isaiah 40:21-24—

Acts 17:26—

Do you normally recognize the Lord's control of all events? If not, how can you become more consistent in recognizing His control?

DAY THREE _____

Read Genesis 45:4-8; Genesis 50:19-20 and Romans 8:28.

Why is it important to realize that God controls and uses even difficult circumstances for good in the life of a godly person?

How does this perspective impact you today?

Share a difficult circumstance you have experienced and how the Lord ultimately used it for good in your life.

DAY FOUR

Read Psalm 34:9-10; Matthew 6:31-33 and Philippians 4:19.

What has the Lord promised concerning meeting your needs?

Give a biblical example of the Lord providing for needs in a supernatural way.

How does this apply to you today?

DAY FIVE

Read the God's Part Notes.

Describe the most important concept in God's Part.

How can you work to be consistent in recognizing the Lord's ownership of your possessions?

What personal benefits do you anticipate from this consistency?

DAY SIX
PONDER YOUR FUTURE

What three goals do you want to accomplish during the next five to ten years?

Describe what financial resources will be required to accomplish your goals. What is your plan to acquire the necessary finances?

As you think of yourself as an older person what do you wish to be remembered for?

In light of your answers to these questions, what actions do you need to take?

 My prayer request for the coming week:

GOD'S PART NOTES

In Scripture God calls Himself by more than 250 names. The name that best describes God's part in the area of money is *Master.* This is the most important section of this entire study because how we view God determines how we live. After losing his children and all his possessions, Job was able to worship God because he knew the Lord and the Lord's role as Master of those possessions. Why did Moses forsake the treasures of Egypt and choose to suffer with the people of God? It was because Moses knew the Lord and accepted His role as Master. There are three facets to God's position as Master.

GOD IS THE OWNER

The Lord owns all our possessions. *"Behold, to the Lord your God belong . . . the earth and all that is in it"* (Deuteronomy 10:14). *"The earth is the Lord's, and all it contains"* (Psalm 24:1).

WHERE DID GOD GET ALL THE FINANCING FOR THIS?

Scripture reveals specific items God owns. Leviticus 25:23 identifies Him as the owner of all the land: *"The land, moreover, shall not be sold permanently, for the land is Mine."* Haggai 2:8 says that He owns the precious metals: *"'The silver is Mine, and the gold is Mine,' declares the Lord of hosts."* And in Psalm 50:10-12, the Scriptures tell us: *"For every beast of the forest is Mine, the cattle on a thousand hills . . . everything that moves in the field is Mine. If I were hungry, I would not tell you; for the world is Mine, and all it contains."*

The Lord is the Creator of all things, and He has never transferred ownership of His creation to people. In Colossians 1:17 we are told that *"in Him all things hold together."* At this very moment the Lord literally holds everything together by His power.

When we acknowledge God's ownership, every spending descision becomes a spiritual descision.

OWNERSHIP OR LORDSHIP?

If we are going to be genuine followers of Christ, we must transfer ownership of all that we have to the Lord. *"So therefore, no one of you can be My disciple who does not give up all his own possessions"* (Luke 14:33). We must give up all claims to the ownership of all that we have. I have found that the Lord will sometimes test us by asking that we be willing to relinquish the very possession that is dearest to us. The most vivid example of this in Scripture is when the Lord asked Abraham to *"take now your son, your only son, whom you love, Isaac . . . and offer him there as a burnt offering"* (Genesis 22:2). When Abraham obeyed, demonstrating his willingness to give up his dearest possession, God responded,

> *Do not stretch out your hand against the lad . . . for now I know that you fear God, since you have not withheld your son, your only son, from Me.*
>
> GENESIS 22:12

When we acknowledge God's ownership, every spending decision becomes a spiritual decision. No longer do we ask, "Lord, what do You want me to do with **my** money?" The question is restated, "Lord, what do You want me to do with **Your** money?" When we have this perspective and prayerfully handle His money according to His wishes, spending and saving decisions are equally as spiritual as giving decisions.

The Lord's ownership also influences how we care for possessions. For example, because the Lord is the owner of my car, I want to please Him by keeping it cleaner and in better repair.

CONTENTMENT

Recognizing the Lord as owner is important in learning contentment. If you believe that you own a particular possession, then the circumstances surrounding that possession have a significant influence on your attitude. If it's a favorable situation, you will be happy. If it's an adverse circumstance, you will be discontent.

Shortly after Jim came to grips with God's ownership, he purchased a new car. He had driven the car for only two days before someone rammed into the side of it. Jim's first reaction was "Lord, I don't know why You want a dent in Your car, but now You've got a big one!" Jim was learning contentment!

RECOGNIZING GOD'S OWNERSHIP

Consistently recognizing God's ownership is difficult. It is easy to believe intellectually that God owns all you have, but yet live as if this were not true. Our culture suggests an opposing view. Everything around us, the media and even the law, says that what

Genuinely acknowledging God's ownership requires nothing less than a total change of perception.

you possess, you and you alone own. Genuinely acknowledging God's ownership requires nothing less than a total change of perception.

Here are a number of practical suggestions to help us recognize God's ownership:

1. For the next thirty days meditate on 1 Chronicles 29:11-12 when you first awake and just before going to sleep;
2. Be careful in the use of personal pronouns; consider substituting "the" or "the Lord's" for "my," "mine" and "ours";
3. Ask the Lord to make you aware of His ownership and to enable you to willingly relinquish ownership. Make this a special object of prayer during the next thirty days;
4. Establish the habit of acknowledging the Lord's ownership every time you purchase an item.

GOD IS IN CONTROL

Besides being Creator and Owner, God is ultimately in control of every event that occurs upon the earth. *"We adore you as being in control of everything"* (1 Chronicles 29:11, LB). *"Whatever the Lord pleases He does, in heaven and in earth"* (Psalm 135:6). And in the book of Daniel, King Nebuchadnezzar stated:

> *I praised the Most High; I honored and glorified Him who lives forever. . . . All the peoples of the earth are regarded as nothing. He does as He pleases with the powers of heaven and the peoples of the earth. No one can hold back His hand or say to Him: "What have you done?"*
>
> DANIEL 4:34-35

The Lord is in control even of difficult events.

> *I am the Lord, and there is no other, the One forming light and creating darkness, causing well-being and creating calamity; I am the Lord who does all these.*
>
> ISAIAH 45:6-7

It is important for the child of God to realize that his heavenly Father orchestrates even seemingly devastating circumstances for ultimate good in the lives of the godly.

> *And we know that God causes all things to work together for good for those who love God, to those who are called according to His purpose.*
>
> ROMANS 8:28

When we learn God's part and then discharge our part faithfully, we can experience contentment.

The Lord allows difficult circumstances for three reasons:

1. He Accomplishes His Intentions. This is illustrated in the life of Joseph who, as a teenager, was sold into slavery by his jealous brothers. Joseph responded correctly to his brothers in this way:

> *Do not be grieved or angry with yourselves, because you sold me here; for God sent me before you to preserve life . . . it was not you who sent me here, but God.*
>
> GENESIS 45:5-8

> *And as for you, you meant evil against me, but God meant it for good in order to bring about this present result, to preserve many people alive.*
>
> GENESIS 50:20

2. He Develops Our Character. Godly character, something that is precious in the sight of the Lord, is often developed in the midst of trying times.

> *We also exult in our tribulations, knowing that tribulation brings about perseverance; and perseverance, proven character.*
>
> ROMANS 5:3-4

3. He Disciplines His Children.

> *For those whom the Lord loves He disciplines . . . He disciplines us for our good, that we may share His holiness. All discipline for the moment seems not to be joyful but sorrowful; yet to those who have been trained by it, afterwards it yields the peaceful fruit of righteousness.*
>
> HEBREWS 12:6,10-11

When we are disobedient, we can expect our loving Lord to administer discipline, often through difficult circumstances, to encourage us to abandon our sin and "share His holiness."

You can be content in knowing that your loving heavenly Father is in control of every situation you will ever face, each of which He intends to use for a good purpose.

> Y ou can be content in knowing that your loving heavenly Father is in control of every situation you will ever face, each of which He intends to use for a good purpose.

GOD IS THE PROVIDER

The Lord promises to provide our needs.

> *But seek ye first the kingdom of God and His righteousness and all these things [food and clothing] shall be added unto you.*
>
> MATTHEW 6:33, KJV

The same Lord who fed manna to the children of Israel during their forty years of wandering in the wilderness and who fed 5,000 with only five loaves and two fish has promised to provide our needs as well. This is the same Lord who told Elijah,

> *I have commanded the ravens to provide for you . . . and the ravens brought him bread and meat in the morning and bread and meat in the evening.*
>
> 1 KINGS 17:4,6

God is both predictable and unpredictable. He is absolutely predictable in His faithfulness to provide for our needs. What we cannot predict is how the Lord will provide. He uses various and often surprising means—an increase in income or a gift. He may provide an opportunity to "stretch" our limited resources through money—saving purchases. Regardless of how He chooses to provide for our needs, He is completely reliable.

The Lord instructs us to be content when our basic needs are met. *"And if we have food and covering, with these we shall be content"* (1 Timothy 6:8).

Charles Allen tells a story illustrating this principle: As World War II was drawing to a close, the Allied armies gathered up many orphans. They were placed in camps where they were fed well. Despite excellent care, they were afraid and slept poorly.

Finally, a psychologist came up with a solution. Each child was given a piece of bread to hold after he was put to bed. If he was hungry, more food was provided, but when he was finished, this particular piece of bread was just to be held—not eaten.

The piece of bread produced wonderful results. The children went to bed knowing instinctively that they would have food to eat the next day. That guarantee gave the children a restful and contented sleep.

Similarly, the Lord has given us His guarantee—our "piece of bread." As we cling to His promises of provision, we can relax and be content. *"And my God shall supply all your needs according to His riches"* (Philippians 4:19).

It is important to understand the distinction between a need and a want. The definition of a need is a basic necessity of life. Our basic necessities of life are food, clothing and shelter. A want is anything in excess of a need. The Lord may allow us to have our wants fulfilled, but He has not guaranteed to provide our every want.

> *The definition of a need is a basic necessity of life. Our basic necessities of life are food, clothing and shelter. A want is anything in excess of a need.*

GETTING TO KNOW GOD

God, as He is revealed in Scripture, is much different than the way people commonly imagine Him to be. Our tendency is to shrink God down and fit Him into a mold with human abilities and limitations. Our failure to recognize God's part is due to the fact that we do not understand the greatness of God, *"who stretched out the heavens and laid the foundations of the earth"* (Isaiah 51:13). We expand our vision to capture the true perspective of God primarily through studying what the Bible tells us about Him. The following are only a few samples:

1. He is Lord of the universe. Carefully review some of His names and attributes: Creator, the Almighty, eternal, all-knowing, all-powerful, omnipresent, awesome, Lord of lords and King of kings.

The Lord's power and ability are incomprehensible. Astronomers estimate there are more than 100 billion galaxies in the universe, each containing billions of stars. The distance from one end of a galaxy to the other is often measured in millions of light years. Though our sun is a relatively small star, it could contain over one million earths, and it sustains temperatures of 27 million degrees Fahrenheit at its center. The enormity of the universe is mind boggling. Isaiah writes,

> *Lift up your eyes on high and see who has created these stars, the One who leads forth their host by number, He calls them all by name; because of the greatness of His might and the strength of His power not one of them is missing.*
>
> ISAIAH 40:26

2. He is Lord of the nations. Examine the Lord's role and position relative to nations and people.

> *Do you not know? Have you not heard? . . . It is He who sits above the vault of the earth, and its inhabitants are like grasshoppers . . . He it is who reduces rulers to nothing, who makes the judges of the earth meaningless. Scarcely have they been planted, scarcely have they been sown, scarcely has their stock taken root in the earth, but He merely blows on them, and they wither.*
>
> ISAIAH 40:21-24

> *Behold, the nations are like a drop from a bucket, and are regarded as a speck of dust on the scales . . . all the nations are as nothing before Him, they are regarded by Him as less than nothing and meaningless.*
>
> ISAIAH 40:15,17

God doesn't fret over nations and their leaders as if He had no power to intervene.

> *He [the Lord] . . . scattered the nations across the face of the earth. He decided beforehand which should rise and fall, and when. He determined their boundaries.*
>
> ACTS 17:26, LB

The Lord's power and ability are incomprehensible. Astronomers estimate there are more than 100 billion galaxies in the universe, each containing billions of stars.

3. He is Lord of the individual. God is not an aloof, impersonal "force." Rather, He is intimately involved with each of us as individuals.

> *You are familiar with all my ways. Before a word is on my tongue You know it completely, O Lord . . . All the days ordained for me were written in your book before one of them came to be.*
>
> PSALM 139:3-4,16, NIV

The Lord is so involved in our lives that He reassures us, *"The very hairs of your head are numbered"* (Matthew 10:30).

God hung the stars in space, fashioned the earth's towering mountains and mighty oceans and determined the destiny of nations. Jeremiah observed correctly: *"Nothing is too difficult for Thee"* (Jeremiah 32:17). Yet God knows when a sparrow falls to the ground. He is the Lord of the infinite and the infinitesimal. Nothing in this study is more important than "catching the vision" of who God is and what His part is in our finances.

GOD'S PART IN CONTENTMENT

The Lord did not design people to carry the yoke of the responsibilities only He is capable of shouldering. Jesus said,

> *Come to Me, all who are weary and heavy-laden, and I will give you rest. Take My yoke upon you . . . for My yoke is easy, and My load light.*
>
> MATTHEW 11:28-30

God has assumed the burdens of ownership, control and provision. That is why His yoke is easy, and we can rest.

God has assumed the burdens of ownership, control and provision. That is why His yoke is easy, and we can rest.

When I first studied God's part, there was nothing that particularly surprised me. I knew all these truths vaguely. My problem was that I did not always live as if they were true. Our culture contributes to this problem. God is thought to play no part in financial matters, and we have, in some measure, been influenced by this view. Another reason for this difficulty is that God is invisible, and anything that is "out of sight" tends to become "out of mind." I get out of the habit of consistently recognizing His ownership, His control and His provision.

After reading about God's part, some jump quickly to the conclusion that little authority or responsibility remains for us. As we begin studying our part next week, we will discover the Lord has indeed entrusted us with great responsibility.

PONDER YOUR FUTURE

At the end of the remaining chapters there will be a section in which you are asked to ponder your future. The purpose of this section is to challenge you to look ahead and begin to think about important issues you will face as you grow older.

The most consistent comment we have received from graduates of the adult Crown study is this: If only I had understood these principles when I was young! You have a priceless opportunity to learn and apply these principles over a lifetime.

One of the most effective concepts in financial planning is to ask the question, "What are my long-term goals?" Answering that question leads you to the question of "How do I achieve those goals?" The answer to this question should lead to practical steps you can take now.

For example, a long-term goal might be to pay off your school loans as soon as possible. The practical step you can take now might be to minimize your loans by securing a part-time job to help pay for tuition.

This week think long-term. Think of yourself as an older person who is nearing death. As you look back on your life, what things would you like to have accomplished? What do you wish to be remembered for? How should you begin to meet the financial requirements necessary for you to accomplish the things most important to you?

Take your time thinking about these issues. Get away to a quiet place where you can pray and ask for God to guide you.

> *You have a priceless opportunity to learn and apply these principles over a lifetime.*

Faithfulness Required—

"Moreover, it is required in stewards that a man be found faithful."

1 CORINTHIANS 4:2, KJV

MEMORIZE
1 CORINTHIANS 4:2, KJV
"Moreover, it is required in stewards that a man be found faithful"

PRACTICAL APPLICATION
Complete the Deed and bring it with you. Two members of your class will witness your deed to help hold you accountable in the recognition of God's ownership. Also complete the Career and Financial Goals practical application.

DAY ONE

Read Genesis 1:26 and Psalm 8:4-6.

What do these verses say about the authority God gave people?

Then read 1 Corinthians 4:2.

According to this verse what is your requirement as a steward?

How would you define a steward?

DAY TWO

Read the parable of the talents in Matthew 25:14-30.

What does the parable illustrate about the following:

1. Our authority as stewards *(Matthew 25:14)*?

2. Our responsibilities?

3. Our being held accountable for our actions *(Matthew 25:19)*?

4. What blessings did the master give to the faithful stewards *(Matthew 25:20-23)*?

5. What other principles are applicable to you?

DAY THREE _____

Read Luke 16:1-2.

Why did the master remove the steward from his position?

Have you observed the Lord removing people from positions of authority because they were unfaithful? If so, describe the circumstances.

How do you think this principle is applicable to you today?

DAY FOUR _____

Read Luke 16:10.

Describe the principle found in this verse.

How does this apply in your situation?

Then read Luke 16:12.

Are we required to be faithful with other people's possessions? What happens if we are not?

How does this apply to you?

DAY FIVE⎯⎯⎯⎯⎯⎯⎯⎯⎯⎯⎯⎯⎯⎯⎯⎯⎯⎯⎯⎯⎯⎯⎯⎯⎯⎯⎯⎯⎯

Read the Our Part Notes.

How have you observed the Lord using money to mold your character?

What strengths have been developed in your character?

What weaknesses in your character still need to be addressed?

DAY SIX
PONDER YOUR FUTURE

Read Psalm 90:12 and Isaiah 40:6-7.

If you remain healthy, how long can you expect to live?

Why do you think the Lord in *Psalm 90:12* encourages us to number the days we think we will live on earth?

Read Romans 14:10-12; 1 Corinthians 3:12-15 and 2 Corinthians 5:9-10.

What will happen to each of us in the future?

Romans 14:10-12 —

1 Corinthians 3:12-15 —

2 Corinthians 5:9-10 —

In your own words contrast the length of your life with eternity.

How will this impact the way you live and spend money?

 My prayer request for the coming week:

OUR PART NOTES

The word that best describes our part is steward. The Greek word for steward is *oikonomos*, which can be translated into the English words "manager" or "supervisor." The position of steward as used in the Bible denotes a person who has full responsibility for all the master's possessions and household affairs.

As we examine Scripture we see that God, as Master, has given us the authority to be stewards over His possessions. *"You made him ruler over the works of your* [the Lord] *hands; you put everything under his feet"* (Psalm 8:6, NIV).

A STEWARD'S RESPONSIBILITY

The extent of a steward's responsibility is summed up in this verse: *"Moreover, it is required in stewards that a man be found faithful"* (1 Corinthians 4:2, KJV). Before we can be faithful, we must know what we are required to do. Just as the purchaser of computer software studies the manufacturer's manual to learn how to properly operate the program, we need first of all to examine the Creator's handbook — the Bible — to determine how He wants us to handle His possessions.

Two elements of our responsibility to be faithful are important to understand:

1. Faithful With Whatever We Are Given. The Lord requires us to be faithful regardless of how much or how little He has entrusted to us. The parable of the talents illustrates this.

> *For it is just like a man about to go on a journey, who called his own slaves, and entrusted his possessions to them. And to one he gave five talents, to another, two, and to another, one, each according to his own ability.*
> MATTHEW 25:14-15

When the master returned, he held each slave accountable for faithfully managing his possessions. The master

As we examine Scripture we see that God, as Master, has given us the authority to be stewards over His possessions.

31

commended the faithful slave who received the five talents:

> *Well done, good and faithful slave; you were faithful with a few things, I will put you in charge of many things, enter into the joy of your master.*
>
> MATTHEW 25:21

Interestingly, the slave who had been given two talents received the identical reward as the slave who had been given the five talents (see Matthew 25:23). The Lord rewards faithfulness, regardless of the amount over which we are responsible.

We are required to be faithful whether we are given much or little. As someone once said, "It's not what I would do if one million dollars were my lot; it's what I am doing with the ten dollars I've got!"

2. Faithful in Every Area. I hope it becomes apparent from the course that God requires us to be a faithful steward in handling 100 percent of our money, not just 10 percent. Unfortunately, many churches have concentrated only on teaching us how to handle 10 percent of our income—the area of giving. And although this area is crucial, by default we have allowed the body of Christ to learn how to handle the other 90 percent from the world's perspective.

As a result of not being equipped to handle money biblically, many Christians have wrong attitudes toward possessions. This causes them to make incorrect financial decisions and to suffer the painful consequences. Hosea 4:6 reads, *"My people are destroyed for lack of knowledge."*

> "*I*t's not what I would do if one million dollars were my lot; it's what I am doing with the ten dollars I've got!"

REWARDS OF A FAITHFUL STEWARD

The faithful steward will enjoy three benefits:

1. You will experience more intimate fellowship with Christ. Remember what the master said to the slave who had been faithful in discharging his financial responsibilities: *"Enter into the joy of your master"* (Matthew 25:21). We have the opportunity to enter into closer, more intimate fellowship with our Lord as we are faithful with the possessions He has entrusted to us.

Someone once told me that the Lord often allows a person to teach a particular subject because that person needs it so desperately! That is certainly true for me. I have never met anyone who had more wrong attitudes toward money or who handled money more contrarily to Scripture than did I. When I began to apply these principles, I experienced a dramatic improvement in my fellowship with the Lord. Each of the financial principles included in this study is intended to draw us closer to Christ.

2. Your character will be developed. Throughout Scripture there is an intimate correlation between the development of a person's character and how he or she handles money. In fact, God uses money to refine our character. David McConaugh explained in *Money the Acid Test,* "Money, most common of temporal things, involves uncommon and eternal consequences. Even though it may be done quite unconsciously, money molds men in the process of getting it, saving it, spending it and giving it. Depending on how you use money, it proves to be a blessing or a curse to its possessor. Either the person becomes master of the money or the money becomes the master of the person. Our Lord takes money, as essential as it is to our common life, and as sordid as it sometimes seems, and makes it a touchstone to test our lives and an instrument to mold people into the likeness of Himself."

You have heard the expression, "Money talks." And it does. You can tell a lot about a person's character by examining his checkbook because we spend our money on the things that are most important to us. Consequently in Scripture money is regarded as an index to a person's true character.

3. Your financial house will be set in order. As we apply the principles of God's economy to our finances, we will begin to get out of debt, spend more wisely, start saving for our future goals and give even more to the work of Christ.

PRINCIPLES OF FAITHFULNESS

There are three principles of faithfulness that are important to understand.

1. If we waste possessions, the Lord will remove us as steward.

There was a certain rich man who had a steward, and this steward was reported to him as squandering his possessions. And he called him and said to him, "What is this I hear about you? Give an account of your stewardship, for you can no longer be steward."

LUKE 16:2

There are two applications from this passage for us. First of all, when we waste our possessions, this becomes public knowledge and creates a poor testimony. *"This steward was reported to him as squandering his possessions."* Secondly, the Lord will remove us as stewards if we squander what He has given us.

A local businessman earned a fortune and then went on an uncontrolled spending spree. Two years later he informed his office staff that he had little left, and everyone would need to economize. Shortly thereafter, he left for a vacation and had his offices, already beautifully decorated, completely renovated at a

You can tell a lot about a person's character by examining his checkbook because we spend our money on the things that are most important to us.

cost of several thousand dollars.

I visited his newly decorated offices during his vacation, and the entire staff was laughing over his unbridled spending habits. I left with the distinct impression the Lord would soon remove this man from the privilege of stewardship over much. Today he is on the verge of bankruptcy. This principle is applicable today. If you waste the possessions entrusted to you, you will not be given more.

2. Character is developed by faithfulness in little things.

He who is faithful in a very little thing is faithful also in much; and he who is unrighteous in a very little thing is unrighteous also in much.

LUKE 16:10

How do you know if a child is going to take good care of his first car? Observe how he cared for his bicycle. How do you know if a salesperson will do a competent job of serving a large client? Evaluate how he served a small client. If we have the character to be faithful with small things, the Lord knows He can trust us with greater responsibilities.

Hudson Taylor said, "Small things are small things, but faithfulness with a small thing is a big thing."

3. Faithfulness is important with the possessions of another. Faithfulness with another's possessions will, in some measure, determine how much God entrusts to you.

And if you have not been faithful in the use of that which is another's, who will give you that which is your own?

LUKE 16:12

This principle is often overlooked. One of the most faithful men I know rented a vehicle from a friend. While driving the vehicle, he was involved in an accident. After explaining the situation to the owner, he took the vehicle to the owner's mechanic and instructed him, "I want you to completely restore this vehicle. Make it better than it was before the accident, and I will be responsible for the bill." What an example of the faithful use of another's possessions!

Are you careless with your school's supplies? Do you waste electricity when you are staying in a motel room? When someone allows you to use something, are you careful to return it in good shape? I am certain some people have not been entrusted with more because they have been unfaithful with the possessions of others.

> *"Small things are small things, but faithfulness with a small thing is a big thing."* —HUDSON TAYLOR

PONDER YOUR FUTURE

Moses wrote,

> *As for the days of our life, they contain seventy years, or if due to strength, eighty years . . . so teach us to number our days, that we may present to Thee a heart of wisdom.*
>
> PSALM 90:10,12

Understanding the brevity of life is important. The Lord tells us to nurture this view so we can gain wisdom. It forces us to ask the question, "What am I going to do with the relatively few remaining days of my life on earth?"

Most people don't address this issue head on, but I want to challenge you to number your days so you can more accurately consider where you are on life's journey. How many days would you have left if you live to age 70? How many days if you live to age 80?

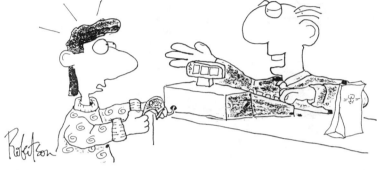

"SORRY CLIFF...BUT THE SENIOR DISCOUNTS ARE NOT FOR THE CLASS OF 1997."

©Andy Robertson

Our culture and the media implore us to focus on the immediate. Advertisers persuade purchasers to gratify themselves today with no thought of tomorrow. However, we need to nurture an eternal perspective.

To better comprehend the reality of eternity, let me share an illustration. If every drop of rain and every flake of snow that have ever fallen along with every grain of sand that has ever existed were each to be counted as a million years, after we've been in heaven for that long, eternity will only have just begun!

OUR TIME HERE ON EARTH

ETERNITY PAST ← → **ETERNITY FUTURE**

To understand the brevity of life, picture our momentary time on earth as but a dot on the time-line of eternity. Yet we have the opportunity to impact eternity by how we handle money and invest our time today.

Gaining eternal perspective and eternal values will have a profound effect on your decision making. Moses is a good example. Study the following carefully:

By faith Moses, when he had grown up, refused to be called the son of Pharaoh's daughter; choosing rather to endure ill treatment with the people of God, than to enjoy the passing pleasures of sin; considering the reproach of Christ greater riches than the treasures of Egypt; for he was looking to the reward.

HEBREWS 11:24-26

Moses faced a choice. As Pharaoh's adopted son he could enjoy the lavish lifestyle of royalty, or he could choose to become a Hebrew slave. Because he had an eternal perspective, he chose the latter and was used by the Lord in a remarkable way. We face a similar decision. We can either live with a view toward eternity or live focused on this present world.

I once visited a field on which I played when I was twelve years old. I remembered it as a huge field surrounded by towering fences. I was shocked to discover how small it really was. I can also remember wanting something so much I could almost taste it. Yet today it means almost nothing to me!

I think we will experience something similar when we arrive in heaven. Many things that seem so large and important to us now will fade into insignificance in the light of eternity.

NOTHING DEPRECIATES A CAR FASTER THAN HAVING YOUR ROOMMATE BUY A NEW ONE.

THE OMNISCIENT GOD

There is nothing you will ever do or think that the Lord does not know. Your life—past, present and future—is an open book to Him.

And there is no creature hidden from His sight, but all things are open and laid bare to the eyes of Him with whom we have to do.

HEBREWS 4:13

And from Psalm 139:1-3:

O Lord, you have searched me and you know me. You know when I sit and when I rise; you perceive my thoughts from afar . . . you are familiar with all my ways (NIV).

The thought of being fully known would be overwhelming if it were not balanced with the knowledge that the Lord also loves us deeply. On my wall hangs a beautiful needlepoint picture created by my wife, Bev, that reads, "The One who knows you best loves you most."

> *Many things that seem so large and important to us now will fade into insignificance in the light of eternity.*

ACCOUNTABILITY AND REWARDS

The Lord will hold us accountable for how we use our time, talent and resources, just as the parable of the talents illustrates: *"Now after a long time the master of those slaves came and settled accounts with them"* (Matthew 25:19). Second Corinthians 5:9-10 reads,

> *Therefore also we have as our ambition . . . to be pleasing to Him. For we must all appear before the judgment seat of Christ, that each one may be recompensed for his deeds in the body, according to what he has done, whether good or bad.*

Each one of us will ultimately stand before the Lord and be asked to account for how we managed our time, money, talent and resources.

This perspective should motivate us to live and to handle money strictly according to the principles of Scripture. Our life on earth is so brief when compared with eternity; yet how we live on earth will influence how we live throughout eternity.

> *Now if any man builds upon the foundation with gold, silver, precious stones, wood, hay, straw, each man's work will become evident; for the day [judgment day] will show it, because it is to be revealed with fire; and the fire itself will test the quality of each man's work . . . if it remains, he shall receive a reward.*
>
> 1 CORINTHIANS 3:12-14

The thought of being fully known would be overwhelming if it were not balanced with the knowledge that the Lord also loves us deeply.

Work Diligently As Unto The Lord—

"Whatever you do, do your work heartily, as for the Lord rather than for men . . . It is the Lord Christ whom you serve."

COLOSSIANS 3:23-24

MEMORIZE COLOSSIANS 3:23-24
Whatever you do, do your work heartily, as for the Lord rather than for men; knowing that from the Lord you will receive the reward of the inheritance. It is the Lord Christ whom you serve"

PRACTICAL APPLICATION
Complete the Resumé and Job Interview practical application.

DAY ONE

Read Genesis 2:15.

Did the Lord first institute work prior to sin entering the world? Why is this important to recognize?

Then read Genesis 3:17-19.

What was the consequence of sin on work?

Then read Exodus 20:9 and 2 Thessalonians 3:10-12.

What do these passages communicate to you about work?

Exodus 20:9—

2 Thessalonians 3:10-12—

DAY TWO

Read Genesis 39:2-5; Exodus 35:30-35; Exodus 36:1-2 and Psalm 75:6-7.

What do each of these verses tell us about the Lord's involvement in our work?

Genesis 39:2-5 —

Exodus 35:30-35 —

Exodus 36:1-2 —

Psalm 75:6-7 —

How do these truths differ from the way people view work at the job or at school?

How will this perspective impact your work?

DAY THREE _____

Read Ephesians 6:5-9; Colossians 3:22-25 and 1 Peter 2:18.

What responsibilities does the employee have according to these verses?

For whom do you really work? How will this understanding alter your work performance?

DAY FOUR _____

Read Proverbs 6:6-11; Proverbs 18:9 and 2 Thessalonians 3:7-9.

What is God's perspective on working hard?

Proverbs 6:6-11 —

Proverbs 18:9 —

2 Thessalonians 3:7-9 —

Do you work hard? If not, describe what steps you will take to improve your work habits.

Then read Exodus 34:21.

What does this verse communicate to you about rest?

Do you get sufficient rest?

How do you guard against overwork?

DAY FIVE_____

Read the *Work Notes* and answer:

What in the notes proved especially interesting or challenging?

How will this impact you?

Do you usually recognize that you are working for the Lord? If not, what will you do to improve this recognition?

Can you name a godly person in Scripture who retired?

Do you think retirement, as it is currently practiced in our culture, is biblically permissible?

What is your view of retirement?

DAY SIX
PONDER YOUR FUTURE

Ephesians 2:10 reads, *"For we are His workmanship, created in Christ Jesus for good works, which God prepared beforehand, that we should walk in them."* Each of us has a specific calling or vocation which the Lord intends for us. He has given us the talents, abilities and spiritual gifts to function well in the vocation He has for us.

List your dominant talents and abilities. (You may want to seek the counsel of those close to you for their assessment.)

Do you have a passionate or deep level of excitement about a particular vocation? If so, describe it.

What steps have you taken to either identify your future vocation or to prepare for it?

Have you identified a potential mentor who is involved in the career you are interested in pursuing? If so, who is it? When will you ask them to share their experience with you?

If you have not identified a potential mentor, what steps will you take to do so?

My prayer request for the coming week:

WORK NOTES

Over a fifty-year span an average person spends 100,000 hours working. Many, however, are dissatisfied with their jobs, because they feel unfulfilled, underpaid, or underappreciated. Perhaps no statistic demonstrates this more than job-hopping tendencies. A recent survey found that the average man changes jobs every four and one-half years, the average woman every three years.

Boredom, lack of fulfillment, fear of losing one's job, inadequate wages and countless other pressures have contributed to this discontentment. Doctors, housewives, secretaries, salesmen, blue collar workers, managers and those in Christian service — regardless of the profession — all have experienced similar frustrations.

Understanding and implementing scriptural principles that relate to work will enable you to find satisfaction in your job. It will also place you in a position where the Lord can prosper you.

We will examine three broad principles of work, explore God's part in work, concentrate on our responsibilities in work, and review several practical work issues.

BIBLICAL PERSPECTIVE OF WORK

Even before the fall, the time at which sin entered the human race, God instituted work. *"The Lord God took the man and put him into the garden of Eden to cultivate it and keep it"* (Genesis 2:15). The very first thing the Lord did with Adam was to put him to work. Despite what many have come to think, work was initiated for man's benefit in the sinless environment of the garden of Eden. Work is not a result of the curse.

After the fall, work was made more difficult.

Cursed is the ground because of you; in toil you shall eat of it all the days of your life. Both thorns and thistles it shall grow for you; and you shall eat the plants of the field; by the sweat of your face you shall eat bread.

GENESIS 3:17-19

NECESSITY OF WORK

Work is so important that in Exodus 34:21 God gives this command: *"You shall work six days."* In the New Testament we discover that Paul is just as direct. *"If anyone will not work, neither let him eat"* (2 Thessalonians 3:10). Examine this verse carefully. It says, *"If anyone **will not** work."* It did not say, *"If anyone **cannot** work."* This principle does not apply to those who are physically or mentally unable to work. It is for those who are able but choose not to work.

A close friend of ours has a sister in her mid-thirties whose parents have always supported her. She has never had to face the responsibilities and hardships involved in a job. As a consequence, her character has not been properly developed, and she is extremely immature in many areas of her life.

One of the primary purposes of work is to develop character. While the carpenter is building a house, the house is also building the carpenter. His skill, diligence and judgment are refined. A job is not merely a task designed to earn money; it's also intended to produce godly character in the life of the worker.

> A job is not merely a task designed to earn money; it's also intended to produce godly character in the life of the worker.

I PREFER DOING BUSINESS OVER THERE — THE KID'S A REAL PERFECTIONIST.

DIGNITY IN ALL WORK

According to Scripture there is dignity in all types of work. Scripture does not elevate any honest profession above another. A wide variety of vocations are represented in the Bible. David was a shepherd and a king. Luke was a doctor. Lydia was a retailer who sold purple fabric. Daniel was a government worker. Paul was a tent-maker and Amos was a fig-picker. If God can use a fig-picker, He can certainly use us in our jobs! And finally, the Lord Jesus was a carpenter.

In God's economy there is equal dignity in the labor of the automobile mechanic and the president of General Motors, in the labor of the leader of a national Christian ministry and a secretary serving in that ministry.

GOD'S PART IN WORK

Scripture reveals three specific responsibilities the Lord has in connection with work.

1. THE SOURCE OF JOB SKILLS

Exodus 36:1 illustrates this truth: *"And every skillful person in whom the Lord has put skill and understanding to know how to perform all the work."* God has given people a wide variety of abilities, manual skills and intellectual capacities. It is not a matter of one person being better than another; it is simply a matter of having received different abilities.

2. THE ORIGIN OF SUCCESS

The life of Joseph is a perfect example of God orchestrating success.

> *The Lord was with Joseph, so he became a successful man . . .*
> *his master saw that the Lord was with him and how the Lord*
> *caused all that he did to prosper in his hand.*
>
> GENESIS 39:2-3

As we have seen, you and I have certain responsibilities, but we need to recognize that it is ultimately God who gives us success.

3. THE SOURCE OF PROMOTION

Psalm 75:6-7 reads, *"For promotion and power come from nowhere on earth, but only from God"* (LB). As much as it may surprise you, your boss is not the one who controls whether or not you will be promoted.

This perspective of God's part in work is a remarkable contrast to the way most people think. Our culture leaves God out of work. People believe they alone are responsible for their job skills and control their success and promotions. However, those with a biblical understanding will approach work with an entirely different frame of reference.

One of the major reasons people experience stress and frustration in their jobs is because they don't understand God's part in work. Stop reading for a few minutes. Think about God's part—He gives you your skills and controls your success and promotion. How should this perspective impact you and your job?

The most important question you need to answer every day as you begin your work is: "For whom do I work?"

OUR PART IN WORK

Scripture reveals we actually are serving the Lord in our work and not people.

> *Whatever you do, do your work heartily, as for the Lord*
> *rather than for men; knowing that from the Lord you will*
> *receive the reward of the inheritance. It is the Lord Christ*
> *whom you serve.*
>
> COLOSSIANS 3:23-24

This perspective has profound implications. Consider your attitude toward work. If you could see the person of Jesus Christ as your teacher or boss, would you strive to be more faithful in your school work or on your job? The most important question you need to answer every day as you begin your work is: "For whom do I work?" You work for Christ.

HARD WORK

"Whatever your hand finds to do, verily do it with all your might" (Ecclesiastes 9:10). *"The precious possession of a man is diligence"* (Proverbs 12:27). In Scripture hard work and diligence are encouraged while laziness is repeatedly condemned: *"He who is slack in his work is brother to him who destroys"* (Proverbs 18:9).

Paul's life was an example of hard work.

> *With labor and hardship we kept working night and day so that we might not be a burden to any of you . . . in order to offer ourselves as a model for you, that you might follow our example.*
>
> 2 THESSALONIANS 3:8-9

Your work should be at such a level that people will never equate laziness and mediocrity with God. Nothing less than hard work and the pursuit of excellence pleases the Lord. We are not required to be "super-workers"—people who never make mistakes. Rather, the Lord expects us to do the best we possibly can.

OVERWORK

A frantic, breathless, over commitment to work pervades our culture. Working hard must be balanced by the other priorities of life. Clearly, our first priority is our relationship with the Lord. *"But seek first His kingdom and His righteousness"* (Matthew 6:33).

If a job demands so much of your time and energy that you neglect these priorities, then you are working too hard. You should determine whether the job is too demanding or your work habits need changing. If you are a "workaholic," take extra precautions to guard against forsaking the other priorities of life.

Exodus 34:21 reads, *"You shall work six days, but on the seventh day you shall rest; even during plowing time and harvest you shall rest."* I believe this Old Testament principle of resting one day out of seven has application for us today. This has been difficult for me, particularly during times of "plowing or harvesting" when a project deadline is approaching, or I am under unusual financial pressure.

Rest can become an issue of faith. Is the Lord able to make our six days of work more productive than seven days? Yes! The Lord instituted this weekly rest for our physical, mental and spir-

"SO MR. PHELPS, WHAT MAKES YOU THINK THAT YOU'RE EXPERIENCING BURNOUT?"

©Andy Robertson

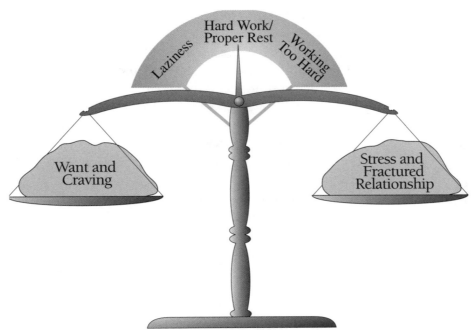

A Balanced Life with Contentment

itual health. Study the diagram at the top of this page to understand the balance God wants in our lives.

EMPLOYEE'S RESPONSIBILITIES

We can identify the six major responsibilities of the godly employee by examining an event in the life of Daniel—the well-known story of Daniel in the lions' den.

In Daniel chapter 6 we are told that Darius, the king of Babylon, appointed 120 men to administer the government and three men, one of whom was Daniel, to supervise these administrators. King Darius decided to promote Daniel to govern the entire kingdom. Daniel's fellow employees then sought to eliminate him. First of all, they looked for an opportunity to discredit him in his job. After this failed, they appealed to King Darius who decreed that everyone in the kingdom would be required to worship only the king or suffer the punishment of death in the lions' den. Daniel was thrown to the lions after refusing to cease worshipping the living God. The Lord then rescued this godly employee by sending His angel to shut the lions' mouths. The six characteristics of a godly employee are:

1. ABSOLUTE HONESTY

Daniel 6:4 tells us that his fellow employees could find no grounds for accusation against Daniel in regard to his job, because there was "*no evidence of corruption*" in Daniel's work. He was absolutely honest. We will study the importance of absolute honesty in Chapter 6.

2. FAITHFULNESS

We discover the second characteristic of the godly employee in Daniel 6:4: *"He was faithful."* The godly employee needs to establish the goal of being faithful and excellent in his work, then to work hard to attain that goal.

3. PRAYERFULNESS

The godly employee is a person of prayer.

> *Now when Daniel knew that the document was signed [restricting worship to the king alone] . . . he continued kneeling on his knees three times a day, praying and giving thanks before his God, as he had been doing previously.*
>
> DANIEL 6:10

Daniel's job was that of governing the most powerful country of his day. Few of us will ever be faced with the magnitude of Daniel's responsibilities and the demands upon his time. Yet he knew the importance and priority of prayer. If you are not praying consistently, your work is suffering.

4. HONORING YOUR EMPLOYER

"Daniel spoke to the king, 'O king live forever!'" (Daniel 6:21). What a remarkable response from Daniel. The king, his employer, had been deceived and was forced to sentence Daniel to the lions' den. Think how natural it would have been to say something like, "You creep! The God who sent His angel to shut the lions' mouths is going to punish you!" But Daniel's reaction was to honor his boss.

The godly employee always honors his superior. First Peter 2:18 reads, *"Servants [employees] be submissive to your masters [employer] with all respect, not only to those who are good and gentle, but also to those who are unreasonable."* One way to honor your employer is to never participate in gossip behind your employer's back, even if he or she is not an ideal person.

5. HONORING FELLOW EMPLOYEES

People will play "office politics" in the never-ending competition for promotion. Some will even try to have you terminated from your job. Daniel was the object of attempted murder by his peers. Despite this, there is no evidence that Daniel did anything but honor his fellow employees. Never slander a fellow employee behind his or her back. *"Do not slander a slave [employee] to his master [employer], lest he curse you and you be found guilty"* (Proverbs 30:10).

> A job well done earns you the right to tell others with whom you work about the reality of Christ.

The godly person should avoid office politics and manipulation to secure a promotion. Your superior does not control your promotion! The Lord Himself makes that determination. We can be content in our job by striving for faithfulness, honoring superiors and encouraging our fellow employees. Having done this, we can know that Christ will promote us if and when He chooses.

6. Verbalizing Your Faith

King Darius would never have known about the living God if Daniel had not communicated his faith verbally at appropriate moments during the normal conduct of his job.

> *The king spoke and said to Daniel, "Daniel, servant of the living God, has your God, whom you constantly serve, been able to deliver you from the lions?"*
>
> DANIEL 6:20

Darius would not have been as powerfully influenced by Daniel sharing his faith if he had not observed this employee fulfilling his responsibilities with honesty and faithfulness. Listen to the words of Darius:

> *I make a decree that in all the dominion of my kingdom men are to fear and tremble before the God of Daniel; for He is the living God and enduring forever, and His kingdom is one which will not be destroyed, and His dominion will be forever.*
>
> DANIEL 6:26

Daniel influenced his employer, one of the most powerful people in the world, to believe in the only true and living God. You have that same opportunity in your own God-given sphere of school and work. Let me say this another way. A job well done earns you the right to tell others with whom you work about the reality of Christ. As we view our work from God's perspective, dissatisfaction will turn to contentment from a job well done, and drudgery will become excitement over the prospect of introducing others to the Savior.

OTHER WORK ISSUES

There are several other important aspects concerning work.

AMBITION

Scripture does not condemn ambition. Paul was ambitious.

The Bible is not the enemy of ambition, only of the wrong type of ambition.

We have as our ambition . . . to be pleasing to Him. For we must all appear before the judgment seat of Christ, that each one may be recompensed for his deeds.

2 CORINTHIANS 5:9-10

What is strongly denounced is selfish ambition.

The Lord will render to every man according to his deeds . . . to those who are selfishly ambitious . . . wrath and indignation.

ROMANS 2:6,8

But if you have . . . selfish ambition in your heart, do not be arrogant and so lie against the truth. This wisdom is not that which comes down from above, but is earthly, natural, demonic. For where . . . selfish ambition exists, there is disorder and every evil thing.

JAMES 3:14-16

But you, are you seeking great things for yourself? Do not seek them.

JEREMIAH 45:5

FRANK'S NOT WHAT YOU'D CALL A MORNING PERSON.

The motivation for our ambition should be a longing to please Christ. We should have as our goal to become an increasingly faithful steward in using the possessions and skills entrusted to us. In our work we should strive to please the Lord by discharging our job responsibilities to the best of our ability.

PARTNERSHIPS

Scripture clearly discourages business partnerships with those who do not know Christ. Second Corinthians 6:14-17 reads,

Do not be bound together [unequally yoked] with unbelievers; for what partnership have righteousness and lawlessness, or what fellowship has light with darkness? Or what harmony has Christ with Belial, or what has a believer in common with an unbeliever? Or what agreement has the temple of God with idols? For we are the temple of the living God; just as God said, "I will dwell in them and walk among them; and I will be their God, and they shall be My people. Therefore, come out from their midst and be separate," says the Lord.

Many have violated this principle and have suffered financially. In my opinion, we should also be very careful before entering into a partnership even with another Christian. I would consider only a few people as potential partners. These are men I have known intimately for years. I have observed their commitment to the Lord, I know their strengths and weaknesses, and I have consistently seen them handle money faithfully. **Do not rush into a partnership!** Prayerfully evaluate what it may entail.

Before forming a partnership, reduce your understandings, assumptions and agreements into written form with your future partner. "But we've been friends for years," you may say. That may be true, but if you really value the relationship, you will protect it from a misunderstanding by putting the details of the agreement down on paper. In this written document provide a method to dissolve the partnership. If you are not able to agree in writing, do not become partners.

PROCRASTINATION

A procrastinator is someone who, because of laziness or fear, has a habit of delaying, postponing, or putting things off until later. What begins as a habit can develop into a serious character flaw.

The Bible has many examples of godly people who were **not** procrastinators, and one of my favorite examples is Boaz. Naomi, the mother-in-law of Ruth, made this comment about Ruth's future husband, Boaz: *"Wait, my daughter, until you know how the matter turns out; for the man will not rest until he has settled it today"* (Ruth 3:18). Boaz clearly had the reputation of a person who was faithful to act promptly.

Here are some practical suggestions to help overcome procrastination: (1) List the things you need to do each day. (2) Prayerfully review and prioritize the list according to the tasks you need to accomplish first. (3) Finish the first task on your list before starting the second. Often that first task is the most difficult or the one you fear the most. (4) Ask the Lord to give you courage, remembering Philippians 4:13, *"I can do all things through Him who strengthens me."*

WIVES WORKING OUTSIDE THE HOME

Most women in college have career plans outside of the home. Single women should consider a career as a means of support. Married women without children are often involved in work outside the home. The most difficult decisions concerning work come when a woman has young children at home.

The trend for wives to work full-time jobs has greatly escalated. In 1947 working husbands outnumbered working wives five to one; now the ratio is less than two to one. Married women work to provide additional income for their families, to express their creativity, or because they enjoy the job environment. Widows and divorcees often must work to provide for the basic needs of their families. A Stanford University study found that wives who work outside the home carry a particularly heavy load of seventy to eighty hours a week with the responsibilities of their job plus household work.

In my opinion, during the children's early formative years it is preferable for the mother to be home whenever the children are home, unless the family finances depend upon her income. Titus 2:4-5 reads, *"Encourage the young women to love their husbands, to love their children, to be sensible, pure, workers at home."* As the children mature, the wife will have increased freedom to pursue work outside the home. Proverbs 31:10-31 reads:

> *An excellent wife . . . does him [her husband] good and not evil all the days of her life. She looks for wool and flax, and works with her hands . . . she brings her food from afar. She rises also while it is still night, and gives food to her household . . . She considers a field and buys it; from her earnings she plants a vineyard . . . She stretches out her hands to the distaff, and her hands grasp the spindle. She extends her hand to the poor . . . She makes coverings for herself; her clothing is fine linen and purple. Her husband is known in the gates, when he sits among the elders of the land. She makes linen garments and sells them, and supplies belts to the tradesmen . . . She looks well to the ways of her household, and does not eat the bread of idleness.*

Proverbs 31 paints a beautiful picture of the working wife living a balanced life with the thrust of her activity toward the home. My opinion is that a wife's work is not so much **in** the home as it is **for** the home. The Bible does not say that a wife should be confined to four walls, but rather involved in activities that relate to the home.

Some women are gifted as homemakers, and there is no more important task than raising godly children. However, other women have the aptitude and desire to work outside the home. Either way, it is a decision that the husband and wife should make prayerfully and with full agreement.

PONDER YOUR FUTURE

Each of us has a specific calling or purpose which the Lord intends for us to fulfill in our work. The root meaning of the word "vocation" has to do with a call to a particular task.

Ephesians 2:10 reads,

> *For we are His workmanship, created in Christ Jesus for good works, which God prepared beforehand, that we should walk in them.*

Study this passage carefully. *"We are His workmanship."* The Amplified Bible says *"We are His handiwork."* Each of us has been created uniquely and given special physical, emotional and mental abilities. You have probably heard the expression, "After the Lord made you, He threw away the mold!" You indeed are uniquely gifted. No one in all of history—past, present or future—is like you.

The passage continues, *"Created in Christ Jesus for good works, which God prepared beforehand that we should walk in them."* The Lord created each of us for a particular job, and He endowed us with the proper skills, aptitudes and desires to accomplish this work.

This calling may be full-time Christian service or a secular job. Often people struggle with whether God wants them to be in business once they commit their lives to Christ. Many feel they are not serving Christ in a significant way if they work in business. Nothing could be further from the truth. The key is for each person to determine God's call for his or her life.

In his book *God Owns My Business*, Stanley Tamm writes, "Although I believe in the application of good principles in business, I place far more confidence in the conviction that I have a call from God. I am convinced that His purpose for me is in the business world. My business is my pulpit." For those who earn a living through secular pursuits, it is a great comfort to know that the "call" of holy vocation carries over into all walks of life. God strategically places His children everywhere!

> *The concept of putting an older but able person "out to pasture" is unbiblical.*

FROM THE WALL STREET JOURNAL—PERMISSION, CARTOON FEATURES SYNDICATE

"I can't retire! I haven't paid off my student loan yet."

RETIREMENT

The dictionary defines retirement as "withdrawal from an occupation or business, to give up or retreat from an active life." The goal of retirement is deeply ingrained in our culture. Many people retire at an arbitrary, pre-determined age and cease all labor in the pursuit of a life filled with leisure.

Scripture gives no examples of people retiring and gives only one direct reference to retirement, which is found in Numbers 8:24-26. The instruction there applied exclusively to the Levites who worked on the tabernacle.

As long as one is physically and mentally capable, there is no scriptural basis for a person retiring and becoming unproductive. The concept of putting an older but able person "out to pasture" is unbiblical. Age is no obstacle in finishing the work the Lord has for you to accomplish. He will provide you with the necessary vigor and stamina. For example, Moses was eighty years old when he began his 40-year adventure leading the children of Israel.

Scripture does imply that the type or the intensity of work may change as we grow older—a shifting of the gears to a less demanding pace in order to become more of an "elder seated at the gate." During this season of life we can actively employ the experience and wisdom gained over a lifetime. If we have sufficient income to meet our needs apart from our job, we may choose to leave the job to invest more time in serving others in whatever capacity the Lord directs.

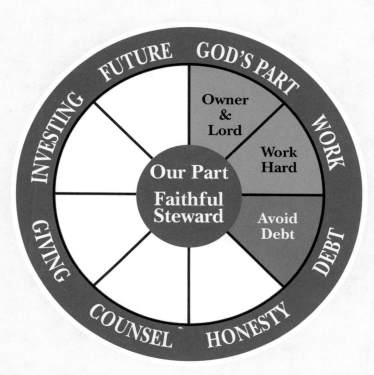

Debt Is Slavery—

*"Just as the rich rule the poor,
so the borrower is servant to the lender."*

PROVERBS 22:7

**MEMORIZE
PROVERBS 22:7**
*"Just as the rich rule the
poor, so the borrower is
servant to the lender."*

**PRACTICAL
APPLICATION**
Complete the Debt List
and the Debt
Repayment Schedule for
each creditor.

DAY ONE _____

Read Deuteronomy 15:4-6; Deuteronomy 28:1-2 ,12 and Deuteronomy 28:15, 43-45.

According to these passages, how was debt viewed in the Old Testament? How is it viewed today?

What was the cause of someone getting in debt (becoming a borrower) or getting out of debt?

DAY TWO _____

Read Romans 13:8; Proverbs 22:7 and 1 Corinthians 7:23.

Is debt encouraged in Scripture? Why?

Romans 13:8—

Proverbs 22:7—

1 Corinthians 7:23—

How does this apply to you?

Do you have a strategy to avoid debt? Do you have a plan to get out of debt? If so, please describe your strategies.

DAY THREE

Read Psalm 37:21 and Proverbs 3:27-28.

What do these verses say about debt repayment and paying current bills?

> *Psalm 37:21—*

> *Proverbs 3:27-28—*

How does this differ from the practices of our culture?

DAY FOUR

Read Proverbs 22:26-27 and Proverbs 17:18.

What does the Bible say about cosigning (striking hands, surety)?

> *Proverbs 22:26-27—*

> *Proverbs 17:18—*

Should parents cosign for their children? Why?

Then read Proverbs 6:1-5.

If someone has cosigned, what should he or she attempt to do?

DAY FIVE

Read the Debt Notes and answer:

What did you learn about debt that proved to be especially helpful?

Why do you think using credit cards can be dangerous for some people?

What will you do to protect yourself from misusing credit cards?

DAY SIX
PONDER YOUR FUTURE

You may purchase a home someday. Before reading about home mortgages on pages 69 to 70 did you understand how much interest you would be required to pay for the mortgage?

Assume you buy a home. Describe how you could minimize the amount of interest you would pay.

My prayer request for the coming week:

DEBT NOTES

To UNDERSTAND THE EXTENT OF DEBT IN OUR COUNTRY, WE will survey government, business and personal debt.

GOVERNMENT DEBT

If you converted the federal debt to one dollar bills, placed them end-to-end, and pointed them out to space, they would extend more than a billion miles . . . beyond the sun! The third largest spending category in the federal budget (behind the military and social programs) is interest on that debt.

BUSINESS DEBT

Corporations owe over $2.5 trillion. Moreover, the *Wall Street Journal* reported that 51 percent of all corporate profits are now being eaten up by interest.

PERSONAL DEBT

Individuals owe more than $3 trillion. The average family spends $400 more than it earns each year. Personal consumer debt increases at the rate of $1,000 per second, and debt has now reached a level where 23 percent of the average person's take-home pay is already committed to payments on existing debt—not including the home mortgage!

Seventy-three percent of college students carry a credit card and the amount of school debt graduates assume is rising rapidly.

We have so much personal debt in our country that the average person has been described as someone driving on a bond-financed highway, in a bank-financed car, fueled by charge-card financed gasoline, going to purchase furniture on the installment plan to put in his savings-and-loan financed home!

And with all this credit floating around, we are bound to have serious financial casualties. In a recent year more than 1,300,000 individuals filed bankruptcy in our country—

*S*tatistics show that people spend approximately one-third more when they use credit cards rather than cash, because they feel they are not really spending money.

"TILL DEBT DO US PART"

more bankruptcies than during the Great Depression. And the most sobering statistic of all: A Gallup Poll found that 56 percent of all divorces are a result of financial tension in the home.

Such financial tension is created largely by believing the "gospel" according to Madison Avenue—buy now and pay later with easy, monthly payments. We all know that there is nothing easy about those monthly payments. Advertisers fail to tell us the whole truth. They leave out one little word—*debt*.

DEFINING DEBT

The dictionary defines debt as: "Money or property which one person is obligated to pay to another." Debt includes money owed to credit card companies, bank loans, student loans, money borrowed from relatives, the home mortgage and past-due medical bills. Bills that come due, such as the monthly phone bill, are not considered debt if they are paid on time.

THE REAL COST OF DEBT

We need to understand the cost of debt. Debt imposes both a financial and physical cost. Assume you have $5,560 in credit-card debt at an 18 percent interest rate. This would cost you about $1,000 in interest annually. Study the chart below.

You can see what lenders have known for a long time—the incredible impact of compounding interest working for you. The lender will accumulate a total of $4,163,213 if you pay him

	Year 5	Year 10	Year 20	Year 30	Year 40
Amount of interest you paid:	$5,000	$10,000	$20,000	$30,000	$40,000
What you would earn on the $1,000 invested at the 12 percent:	6,353	17,549	72,052	214,333	767,091
How much the lender earns from your payment at 18 percent interest:	7,154	23,521	146,628	790,948	4,163,213

$1,000 a year for forty years, and he earns 18 percent on your payment! Is there any wonder credit card companies are eager for you to become one of their borrowers?

Now compare the $40,000 you paid in interest over forty years with the $767,091 you could have accumulated, earning 12 percent on $1,000 each year: $767,091 yields a monthly income of $7,671 if it's earning 12 percent—without ever touching the principal.

Stop to consider this: When a person assumes debt of $5,560 and pays $1,000 a year in interest, if he can earn 12 percent, he actually costs himself $767,091 over forty years. Debt has a much higher cost than many realize. Next time you are tempted to purchase something with debt, ask yourself if the long-term benefits of staying out of debt outweigh the short-term benefits of the purchase

Debt also often increases stress, which contributes to mental, physical and emotional fatigue. It can stifle creativity and devastate relationships. Many people raise their lifestyle through debt, only to discover that the burden of debt then controls their lifestyle. The bumper sticker that reads, "I owe, I owe, it's off to work I go," is an unfortunate reality for too many people.

DEBT IN SCRIPTURE

Scripture's perspective of debt is clear. Carefully read the first portion of Romans 13:8 from several different Bible translations: *"Owe no man anything"* (KJV). *"Let no debt remain outstanding"* (NIV). *"Pay all your debts"* (LB). *"Owe nothing to anyone"* (NAS). *"Keep out of debt and owe no man anything"* (Amplified).

1. Debt is slavery. In Proverbs 22:7 we learn why our Lord speaks so directly to the area of debt: *"Just as the rich rule the poor, so the borrower is servant to the lender"* (LB). When we are in debt, we are in a position of servitude to the lender. And the deeper we are in debt, the more of a servant we become. We do not have the freedom to decide where to spend our income, because our money is already legally obligated to meet these debts.

In 1 Corinthians 7:23 Paul writes, *"You were bought with a price; do not become slaves of men."* Our Father made the ultimate sacrifice by giving His Son, the Lord Jesus Christ, to die for us. And He now wants His children free to serve Him, and not people, in whatever way He chooses.

2. Debt was considered a curse. In the Old Testament being out of debt was one of the promised rewards for obedience.

> *Now it shall be, if you will diligently obey the Lord your God, being careful to do all His commandments which I command you today, the Lord your God will set you high above all the nations of the earth. And all these blessings shall come upon you and overtake you, if you will obey the Lord your God . . . and you shall lend to many nations, but you shall not borrow.*
>
> DEUTERONOMY 28:1-2,12

"Just as the rich rule the poor, so the borrower is servant to the lender." (PROV. 22:7, LB)

However, indebtedness was one of the curses inflicted for disobedience.

> *But it shall come about, if you will not obey the Lord your God, to observe to do all His commandments and His statutes which I charge you today, that all these curses shall come upon you and overtake you . . .The alien who is among you shall rise above you higher and higher, but you shall go down lower and lower. He shall lend to you, but you shall not lend to him; he shall be the head, and you shall be the tail.*
>
> DEUTERONOMY 28:15,43-44

3. Debt presumes upon tomorrow. When we get into debt, we assume that we will earn enough in the future to pay the debt. Scripture cautions us against presumption:

> *Come now, you who say, "Today or tomorrow, we shall go to such and such a city, and spend a year there and engage in business and make a profit." Yet you do not know what your life will be like tomorrow. You are just a vapor that appears for a little while and then vanishes away. Instead, you ought to say, "If the Lord wills, we shall live and also do this or that."*
>
> JAMES 4:13-15

4. Debt may deny God an opportunity. Ron Blue, an outstanding author, tells of a young man who wanted to go to seminary to become a missionary. The young man had no money and thought the only way he could afford seminary was to secure a student loan. However, this would have encumbered him with $40,000 of debt by the time he graduated, which would have been impossible to pay back on a missionary's salary.

After a great deal of prayer, he decided to enroll without the help of a student loan and to trust the Lord to meet his needs. He graduated without borrowing anything and grew in his appreciation for how God could creatively provide his needs. This was the most valuable lesson learned in seminary as he prepared for life on the mission field. Borrowing may deny God an opportunity to demonstrate His reality.

BORROWING

Scripture is silent on the subject of when we can owe money. In my opinion it is possible to owe money for a home mortgage, for your business or for your vocation. This is permissible, I believe, only if the following three criteria are met:

1. The item purchased is an asset with the potential to appreciate or produce an income.

When we get into debt, we asume that we will earn enough in the future to pay the debt.

2. The value of the item equals or exceeds the amount owed against it.

3. The debt should not be so high that repayment puts undue strain on the budget.

Let me give you an example of how a home mortgage might qualify. Historically, the home has usually been an appreciating asset, so it meets the first criterion. If you invest a reasonable down payment, you could expect to sell the home for at least enough to satisfy the mortgage, and this meets the second requirement. Lastly, the monthly house payment should not strain your budget.

If you meet all the criteria and assume some "possible debt," I pray you will immediately establish the goal of eliminating even this debt. There is no assurance that the housing market will appreciate or even maintain current values. A loss of job can interrupt your income. Please consider paying off all debt.

Ziggy/Tom Wilson. Used by permission. United Press Syndicate.

GETTING OUT OF DEBT

There are nine steps for getting out of debt. The steps are easy, but following them requires *hard work*. The goal is D-Day—Debtless Day—when you become absolutely free of debt.

1. Pray for the Lord's help. The first and most important step is to pray. Seek the Lord's help and guidance in your journey toward Debtless Day. A trend is emerging. As people begin to eliminate debt and to accelerate debt repayment, the Lord has blessed their faithfulness. Even if you can afford only a small monthly prepayment of your debt, please do it. The Lord can multiply your efforts.

2. Establish a written budget. In my experience, few people in debt have been using a written budget. They may have had one—neatly filed away in a drawer—but they have not been using it. A written budget helps you plan ahead, analyze your spending patterns and control the biggest budget buster of them all—impulse spending.

3. List everything you own. Evaluate your assets to determine if there is anything you do not need that might be sold to help you get out of debt more quickly. What about that jet ski you no longer use? How about that set of golf clubs gathering dust in the garage? What other assets can you sell that will help you get out of debt?

4. List everything you owe. Many people, particularly if they owe a lot of money, do not know exactly what they owe. List your debts to determine your current financial situation. You also need to determine the interest rate your creditors are charging for each debt.

5. Establish a debt repayment schedule. Part of the practical application this week is establishing a repayment schedule for each debt. I suggest you decide which debts to pay off first based on two factors:

Pay off small debts. Focus on paying off the smallest debts first. You will be encouraged as they are eliminated, and this will free up cash to apply against other debts. After you pay off the first debt, apply its payment toward the next debt you wish to retire. After the second debt is paid off, apply what you were paying on the first and second debts toward the next debt you wish to eliminate, and so forth.

Pay off higher interest rate debts. Determine what rate of interest you are being charged on each debt, and try to pay off first those that charge the highest rate. If you call your credit card company to set up an accelerated debt payment schedule, you will often be able to negotiate a reduced interest rate.

6. Consider earning additional income. Many students hold jobs that simply do not produce enough income to meet their needs, even if they spend wisely. If you earn additional income, decide in advance to pay off debts with the added earnings. We tend to spend more than we make, whether we earn much or little. Spending always seems to keep ahead of earning.

7. Control the use of credit cards. An avalanche of 2.5 billion solicitations a year offering credit cards is overwhelming our mailboxes. Many of these solicitations are deceptive, promising low interest rates, which in the fine print rise to exorbitant levels within a few months. Others offer free T-shirts or such giveaways in an effort to attract our attention.

I do not believe that credit cards are inherently sinful, but they are extremely dangerous. The leading problem college counselors are asked about is the inability of students to handle credit card debt. It is estimated that people carry over 800,000,000 credit cards, and only 40 percent of them are paid in full each month. Statistics show that people spend approximately one-third more when they use credit cards rather than cash, because they feel they are not really spending money (because it's just plastic). As one shopper said to another, "I like credit cards lots more than money, because they go so much further!"

When I analyze the financial situation of someone in debt, I use a simple rule of thumb to determine whether credit cards are too dangerous for them. If they do not pay the entire balance due at the end of each month, I encourage them to perform some plastic surgery—any good scissors will do.

8. Be content with what you have. We live in a culture whose advertising industry has devised powerful, sophisticated methods of inducing the consumer to buy. Frequently the message is intended to create discontentment with what we have.

A clear example is the American company that opened a new plant in Central America because the labor was plentiful

> • *The more television you watch, the more you spend.*
> • *The more you look at catalogues and magazines, the more you spend.*
> • *The more you shop, the more you spend.*

and inexpensive. Everything was progressing smoothly until the villagers received their first paycheck; afterwards they did not return to work. Several days later, the manager went down to the village chief to determine the cause of this problem. The chief responded, "Why should we work? We already have everything we need." The plant stood idle for two months until someone came up with the bright idea of sending a mail-order catalog to every villager. There has never been an employment problem since!

Note these three realities of our consumer driven society:

1. The more television you watch, the more you spend.
2. The more you look at catalogs and magazines, the more you spend.
3. The more you shop, the more you spend.

9. Do not give up! The last step is the most difficult one in getting out of debt. It takes hard work. You must lower your standard of living three times: (a) you must stop spending more than you are making, (b) you must pay interest on the debt, and (c) you must pay back what you have borrowed.

It is never easy to get out of debt, but the freedom is worth the struggle.

It is never easy to get out of debt, but the freedom is worth the struggle.

ESCAPING THE AUTO DEBT TRAP

Automobile loans are one of the leading causes of indebtedness. Seventy percent of all automobiles are financed. The average person keeps his car between three and four years. The average car lasts for ten years.

Here's how to escape this trap. First of all, decide in advance to keep your car for at least six years. Secondly, pay off your automobile loan. Thirdly, continue paying the monthly car payment, but to yourself into a special savings account. Then when you are ready to replace your car, the saved cash plus the trade-in should be sufficient to buy your car without credit. It may not be a new car, but you should be able to purchase a good, low-mileage used car, without any debt.

DEBT REPAYMENT RESPONSIBILITIES

Many delay payments to use the creditor's money as long as possible. There are seminars that actually teach people to live on the "ragged edge of being a dead beat," but this is not biblical.

Do not withhold good from those to whom it is due, when it is in your power to do it. Do not say to your neighbor, "Go, and come back, and tomorrow I will give it," when you have it with you.

PROVERBS 3:27-28

"*The wicked borrows and does not pay back, but the righteous is gracious and gives.*"
(Psalm 37:21)

Godly people should pay their debts and bills as promptly as they can. We have a policy of trying to pay each bill the same day we receive it to demonstrate to others that knowing Jesus Christ has made us financially responsible.

USING YOUR SAVINGS

It is wise not to deplete all your savings to pay off debt. Maintain a reasonable level of savings to provide for the unexpected. If you apply all your savings against debt and the unexpected does occur, you will probably be forced to incur more debt to fund the emergency.

BANKRUPTCY

A court can declare a person bankrupt and unable to pay his debts. Depending upon the type of bankruptcy, the court will either allow the debtor to develop a plan to repay his creditors, or the court will distribute his property among the creditors as payment for the debts.

An epidemic of bankruptcy is sweeping our country. Should a godly person declare bankruptcy? The answer is generally no. Psalm 37:21 tells us, "*The wicked borrows and does not pay back, but the righteous is gracious and gives.*"

In my opinion, bankruptcy is permissible under two circumstances: a creditor forces a person into bankruptcy, or a counselor believes the debtor's emotional health is at stake because of inability to cope with the pressure of unreasonable creditors.

After a person goes through bankruptcy, he should seek counsel from an attorney to determine if it's legal to attempt to repay the debt when he is not obligated to do so. If it is within the law, he should make every effort to repay the debt. For a large debt, this may be a long-term goal that is largely dependent upon the Lord's supernatural provision.

COSIGNING

Cosigning relates to debt. Anytime you cosign, you become legally responsible for the debt of another. It is just as if you went to the bank, borrowed the money and gave it to your friend or relative who is asking you to cosign.

A Federal Trade Commission study found that fifty percent of those who cosigned for bank loans ended up having to make the payment themselves. Seventy-five percent of those who cosigned for finance company loans ended up making the payments! Unfortunately, few cosigners plan for default. The casualty rate is so high because the professional lender has already determined that the loan on its own merit is a bad risk. That is why he won't make the loan without someone who is financially responsible to guarantee its repayment.

Fortunately, Scripture speaks very clearly about cosigning. Proverbs 17:18 reads, *"It is poor judgment to cosign another's note, to become responsible for his debts"* (LB). The words "poor judgment" are better translated "destitute of mind!" Please use sound judgment and never cosign a note or become surety for any debt.

> *"It is poor judgment to cosign another's note, to become responsible for his debts"* (PROV. 17:18, LB)

PONDER YOUR FUTURE

HOME MORTGAGES

A 30-year home mortgage, at a 10 percent interest rate, will require you to pay more than **three times** the amount originally borrowed.

If you plan to purchase a home in the future, I would like to encourage you to pay it off more rapidly than it is scheduled.

When Bev and I first began to understand God's financial principles, we felt we were to pay off everything, including the home mortgage. We began to explore how we might accomplish this.

Let's examine the payment schedule for a home mortgage. Please do not let the size of the mortgage or the rate of interest hinder your thinking; this is for illustration purposes only. In the chart on page 70 we are assuming a $75,000 mortgage at a 12 percent interest rate, paid over 30 years. The first year of the payment schedule (also known as an amortization schedule) would look like the chart.

Original mortgage amount	$100,000.00
Monthly mortgage payment at 10 percent interest	$877. 57
Months paid	x 360
Total payments	$315,925.20

As you can see, the payments during the early years are almost all interest. Out of the total of $9,257.64 in house payments made this first year, only $272.26 went toward principal reduction! In fact, it will be 23½ years before the principal and the interest portions of the payment equal each other! I don't know about you, but a 30-year goal to pay off my home mortgage doesn't excite me. If this can be reduced to 15 years, then the goal becomes much more attainable. There are several methods we can use to pay off the mortgage in half the time.

One method is to increase the amount of your monthly payment. In our example, a $75,000 mortgage at 12 percent interest payable over 30 years requires a monthly installment of $771.47. If you increase the monthly payment by $128.70 to $900.17, the mortgage will be fully paid in fifteen years. You will save $138,864 in interest over the life of your mortgage.

A second method is to prepay the next month's principal payment in addition to your regular monthly payment of $771.47. By doing this consistently for fifteen years you will have paid off the entire mortgage. Obviously, during the early years, the additional payment is low, but in the later years the extra payment will become substantial.

Payment #	Month	Payment	Interest	Principal	Principal Balance
1	Jan.	771.47	750.00	21.47	74,978.53
2	Feb.	771.47	749.79	21.68	74,956.85
3	Mar.	771.47	749.57	21.90	74,934.95
4	Apr.	771.47	749.35	22.12	74,912.83
5	May	771.47	749.13	22.34	74,890.49
6	June	771.47	748.90	22.57	74,867.92
7	July	771.47	748.68	22.79	74,845.13
8	Aug.	771.47	748.45	23.02	74,822.11
9	Sep.	771.47	748.22	23.25	74,798.86
10	Oct.	771.47	747.99	23.48	74,775.38
11	Nov.	771.47	747.78	23.69	74,751.69
12	Dec.	771.47	747.52	23.95	74,727.74
Totals for year:		**9,257.64**	**8,985.38**	**272.26**	

You must study your mortgage to make certain that the mortgage may be prepaid without penalty. A home mortgage usually allows such prepayment. And finally, let your lender know what you are planning. Not many borrowers prepay their mortgages, so he may be in shock for a while!

There are two primary arguments against this: (1) Why pay off a low-interest home mortgage when you can earn more elsewhere? (2) You are losing a tax shelter because the interest paid on a home mortgage is a tax deduction.

Rather than addressing these arguments directly, we should recognize that our tax system is structured partially to reward indebtedness and penalize savings. We are taxed on interest earned, while interest paid on a home mortgage is treated as a tax deduction. However, in spite of our tax structure, the Bible encourages savings and discourages debt. Our purpose is simply to challenge you to seek Christ with an

"YES, WE'D LIKE TO TALK TO YOU ABOUT A HOME EQUITY LOAN FOR OUR DAUGHTER'S PROM DRESS."

©Andy Robertson

open heart to learn what He wants you to do.

For Bev and me, this turned into an exciting time as we began to pay off our mortgage. The Lord provided additional funds for us in an unexpected way, and today we do not owe anyone anything. This allowed me to take time off from my work to study and develop the Crown Ministries materials. God may have something similar for you.

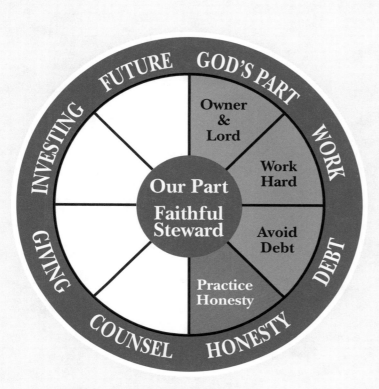

Absolute Honesty Required—

"You shall not steal, nor deal falsely, nor lie to one another."

LEVITICUS 19:11

**MEMORIZE
LEVITICUS 19:11**
"You shall not steal, nor deal falsely, nor lie to one another"

**PRACTICAL
APPLICATION**
Complete the
Estimated Budget
practical
application.

DAY ONE _____

Read Leviticus 19:11-13; Deuteronomy 25:13-16; Ephesians 4:25 and 1 Peter 1:15-16.

What do these verses communicate to you about God's demand for honesty?

Leviticus 19:11-13 —

Deuteronomy 25:13-16 —

Ephesians 4:25 —

1 Peter 1:15-16 —

Are you consistently honest in even the smallest details? If not, how do you propose to change?

What are two factors that motivate or influence us to act dishonestly?

1.

2.

How does this apply to you?

DAY TWO_____ 75

Read Proverbs 14:2 and answer:

Can you practice dishonesty and still love God? Why?

Then read Proverbs 26:28 and Romans 13:9-10.

According to these passages, can you practice dishonesty and still love your neighbor? Why?

DAY THREE _____

Read Psalm 15:1-5; Proverbs 12:22; Proverbs 20:7 and Isaiah 33:15-16 and answer:

What are some of the benefits of honesty?

Psalm 15:1-5 —

Proverbs 12:22 —

Proverbs 20:7 —

Isaiah 33:15-16 —

Then read Proverbs 3:32; Proverbs 13:11 and Proverbs 21:6.

What are some of the curses of dishonesty?

Proverbs 3:32 —

Proverbs 13:11 —

Proverbs 21:6 —

DAY FOUR

Read Exodus 22:1-4; Numbers 5:5-8 and Luke 19:8 and answer:

What does the Bible say about restitution?

If you have acquired anything dishonestly, how will you make restitution?

DAY FIVE

Read the Honesty Notes and answer:

How does the example of Abraham in *Genesis 14:21-23* challenge you to be honest?

Describe any ways you are tempted to be dishonest in small matters.

Then read Exodus 23:8; Proverbs 15:27 and Proverbs 29:4.

What is the biblical position on bribes? Have you ever been asked to give or take a bribe? If so, describe what happened.

DAY SIX
PONDER YOUR FUTURE

Read Exodus 18:21-22 and answer:

Does the Lord require honesty for leaders? Why?

Then read Proverbs 28:16 and Proverbs 29:12.

What are the consequences of dishonesty for people in leadership?

Proverbs 28:16—

Proverbs 29:12—

Have you ever had to interface with a dishonest leader? If so, how did you feel?

Are you currently in a position of leadership? If so, describe benefits you would experience as a leader for being totally honest.

Think of future leadership positions you aspire to hold (in parenting, in business, in education, in church, or in ministry). Describe the character qualities that these positions require.

 My prayer request for the coming week:

HONESTY NOTES

All of us have to make daily decisions about whether or not to handle money honestly. Do we tell the cashier at the grocery store when we receive too much change? Have you ever tried to sell something and been tempted not to tell the whole truth because you might have lost the sale?

HONESTY IN SOCIETY

'All along I thought our level of corruption fell within community standards.'

These decisions are made more difficult because we live in what has been called the "Age of the Rip-off." It is an age in which employee theft is approaching $1 billion a week! It is an age in which an estimated 20 percent of the gross national product is unreported to the government! It is an age in which almost everyone around us seems to be acting dishonestly.

After pumping five dollars' worth of gas in my truck, I asked for a receipt, and the attendant made the receipt for ten dollars. When I pointed out the discrepancy, he replied, "Oh, just turn in the receipt to your company, and you'll make a fast five bucks. After all, that's what many of the mailmen do in this area."

When I heard that, my heart sank. The verse that came immediately to mind was Judges 17:6, *"Every man did what was right in his own eyes."* That is precisely where we are today. We live in an age of "relative" honesty in which people formulate their own standards of honesty that change depending upon their circumstances.

HONESTY IN SCRIPTURE

This practice of relative honesty is in sharp contrast to the unchanging standard we find in Scripture. God demands absolute honesty. Proverbs 20:23 reads, *"The Lord loathes all cheating and dishonesty"* (LB). And Proverbs 12:22 states, *"Lying lips are an abomination to the Lord."* And from Proverbs 6:16-17 we read, *"The Lord hate . . . a lying tongue."*

This practice of relative honesty is in sharp contrast to the unchanging standard we find in Scripture.

© The New Yorker Collection, etc.

Study the comparison below between what the Scriptures teach and what our society practices concerning honesty.

THE GOD OF TRUTH

Truthfulness is one of God's eternal and unchangeable attributes. He is repeatedly identified as the God of truth. *"I am . . . the truth"* (John 14:6). Moreover, the Lord commands us to reflect His honest and holy character: *"Be holy yourselves also in all your behavior; because it is written, 'You shall be holy, for I am holy'"* (1 Peter 1:15-16).

ISSUE	SCRIPTURE	SOCIETY
Standard of honesty:	Absolute	Relative
God's concern about honesty:	He demands honesty	There is no God
The decision to be honest or dishonest is based upon:	Faith in the invisible living God	Only the facts that can be seen
Question usually asked deciding whether to be honest:	Will it please God?	Will I get away with it?

In stark contrast to God's nature, John describes the devil's character:

> He [the devil] was a murderer from the beginning, and does not stand in the truth, because there is no truth in him. Whenever he speaks a lie, he speaks from his own nature; for he is a liar, and the father of lies.
>
> JOHN 8:44

The Lord wants us to become conformed to His honest character rather than to the dishonest nature of the devil.

ABSOLUTE HONESTY

God has imposed the standard of absolute honesty for Christians for the following reasons:

1. We cannot practice dishonesty and love God. Two of the Ten Commandments specifically address honesty. *"You shall not steal. You shall not bear false witness against your neighbor"* (Exodus 20:15-16). And Jesus told us, *"If you love Me, you will keep My commandments"* (John 14:15).

According to Scripture, we cannot practice dishonesty and still love God. A dishonest person acts as if the living God does not even exist! We believe that God is not able to provide what we need, even though He has promised to do so (Matthew 6:33). We decide to take things into our own hands and do it our own dishonest way.

A dishonest person is also acting as if God is incapable of discovering our dishonesty and is powerless to discipline us. If we really believe God will discipline us, then we will not consider acting dishonestly.

Honest behavior is an issue of faith. An honest decision may look foolish in light of the circumstances we can observe. But the godly person has mastered the art of considering another fact which is valid, even though invisible: the person of Jesus Christ. Every honest decision affirms and strengthens our faith in the living God and helps us grow into a closer relationship with Christ. However, if we choose to be dishonest and to walk by sight rather than by faith, we essentially deny our Lord and violate the first and greatest commandment. It is impossible to love God with all our heart, soul and mind, if at the same time, we are dishonest and act as if He does not exist. Scripture declares that the dishonest hate God.

> *He who walks in his uprightness fears the Lord, but he who is crooked in his ways despises Him.*
>
> PROVERBS 14:2

2. We cannot practice dishonesty and love our neighbor. The Lord demands absolute honesty because dishonest behavior also violates the second commandment, *"Thou shalt love thy neighbor as thyself"* (Mark 12:31, KJV). Romans 13:9-10 reads, *"If you love your neighbor as much as you love yourself, you will not want to harm or cheat him, or kill him or steal from him . . . love does no wrong to anyone"* (LB).

When we act dishonestly, we are stealing from another person. We may deceive ourselves into thinking it is a business, the government, or an insurance company that is suffering loss, but if we look at the bottom line, it is the business owners, fellow taxpayers, or the policy holders from whom we are stealing. It is just as if we took the money from their wallets. Dishonesty always injures people. The victim is always a person.

3. Honesty creates credibility for evangelism. Our Lord demands absolute honesty in handling money to enable us to demonstrate the reality of Jesus Christ to those who do not yet know Him.

I will never forget the first time I told a neighbor how he could come to know Christ as his personal Savior. His face turned scarlet as he snarled, "Well, I know a businessman who always goes to church and talks a lot about Jesus. But watch out if you ever get in a business deal with him. He'd cheat his own grandmother. If that's what it means to be a Christian, I don't want any part of it!" Our actions speak louder than our words.

It is impossible to love God with all our heart, soul and mind, if at the same time we are dishonest and act as if He does not exist.

Prove yourselves to be blameless and innocent, children of God above reproach in the midst of a crooked and perverse generation, among whom you appear as lights in the world.

PHILIPPIANS 2:15

We can influence people **for** Jesus Christ by handling our money honestly. Robert Newsom had been trying to sell an old pickup truck for months. Finally, an interested buyer decided to purchase the truck. However, at the last moment he said, "I'll buy this truck, but only on one condition—that you don't report this sale so I won't have to pay state sales tax."

Although he was tempted to comply with the demand, Robert responded, "I'm sorry, but I can't do that because Jesus Christ is my Lord." Robert later said, "You should have seen that man's reaction. He almost went into shock! Then an interesting thing happened. His attitude completely changed. Not only did he purchase the truck, but he eagerly joined my wife and me around our dinner table. Rarely have I seen anyone as open to the truth about knowing Jesus Christ in a personal way."

Because Robert had acted honestly even though it was going to cost him money (*"Prove yourselves to be blameless and innocent, children of God above reproach"*), he had demonstrated to this person (*"a crooked and perverse generation"*) the reality of a personal faith in Jesus Christ (*"appear as lights in the world"*).

4. Honesty confirms God's direction. Proverbs 4:24-26 reads,

Put away from you a deceitful mouth, and put devious lips far from you. Let your eyes look directly ahead, and let your gaze be fixed straight in front of you. Watch the path of your feet and all your ways will be established.

What a tremendous principle. As you are absolutely honest, *"all your ways will be established."* Choosing to walk the narrow path of honesty eliminates the many possible avenues of dishonesty. Decision-making becomes simpler because the honest path is a clear path.

MAJOR DECISIONS

From time to time we all struggle with major decisions. What vocation should I pursue? Should I apply to this graduate school? Honesty helps confirm God's direction in the major decisions.

"If only I had understood that truth," Raymond wept. "But Donna and I wanted that house so much. It was our dream home. However, our existing debts were so large that we couldn't qualify for the mortgage. The only way for us to buy the house was to conceal some of our debts from the bank.

"It was the worst decision of my life. Almost immediately we

> *Choosing to walk the narrow path of honesty eliminates the many possible avenues of dishonesty.*

were unable to meet the house payment and pay our other debts too. The pressure built and was almost more than Donna could stand. Our dream house ended up causing a family nightmare. I not only lost the home, but nearly lost my wife."

Had Raymond and Donna been honest, the bank would not have approved the loan. They would not have been able to purchase that particular home. Had they prayed and waited, perhaps the Lord would have brought something more affordable, thus avoiding the pressure that almost ended their marriage. Honesty helps confirm God's direction.

5. Even the smallest act of dishonesty is devastating. God requires us to be absolutely honest, because even the smallest act of dishonesty is sin. And even the smallest sin interrupts our fellowship with the Lord and retards our maturity in Christ. The smallest "white lie" will harden our hearts, making our consciences increasingly insensitive to sin and deafening our ears to the still small voice of the Lord. This single cancer cell of small dishonesty multiplies and spreads to greater dishonesty. *"Whoever is dishonest with very little, will also be dishonest with much"* (Luke 16:10, NIV).

An event in Abraham's life has challenged me to be honest in small matters. In Genesis 14 the king of Sodom offered Abraham all the goods Abraham recovered when he returned from successfully rescuing the people of Sodom. But Abraham responded to the king,

> *I have sworn to the Lord God Most High, possessor of heaven and earth, that I will not take a thread or a sandal thong or anything that is yours.*
>
> GENESIS 14:22-23

Just as Abraham was unwilling to take so much as a thread or a sandal thong, I challenge you to make a similar commitment in this area of honesty. Covenant not to steal a stamp or a meal or a paper clip or a long distance telephone call or a penny from your school, your employer, or anyone else. The people of God must be honest in even the smallest, seemingly inconsequential matters.

THE TEMPTATION OF DISHONESTY

A friend of mine was teaching these principles to a college class when one student raised his hand, "I think we all would like to be the person you're talking about," said the student. "But I know in my heart that if the right opportunity comes along, I'm going to be dishonest." I think he is correct. Apart from denying ourselves and living our lives yielded to the Holy Spirit, all of us will be dishonest.

Live by the Spirit, and you will not gratify the desires of the sinful nature. For the sinful nature desires what is contrary to the Spirit, and the Spirit what is contrary to the sinful nature.

GALATIANS 5:16-17, NIV

The character of our human nature is to act dishonestly. *"Out of men's hearts come evil thoughts . . . theft . . . deceit"* (Mark 7:21-22, NIV). The desire of the Spirit is for us to be absolutely honest. I can't overemphasize that the absolutely honest life is supernatural. We must submit ourselves entirely to Jesus Christ as Lord and allow Him to live His life through us. There is no other way.

I heartily recommend you read a short book by Andrew Murray entitled *Humility*. It is an excellent and motivating study for living your life yielded to Christ as Lord.

> *A*part from denying ourselves by living our lives yeilded to the Holy Spirit, all of us will be dishonest.

THE GOLDEN RULE

"Do not merely look out for your own personal interests but also for the interests of others" (Philippians 2:4). This verse is better translated, "look intently" after the interests of others. The Lord confronted me through this passage and pointed out my self-centeredness and lack of concern for others just when I was about to purchase some land.

The seller knew nothing of its value. I had been secretly congratulating myself because I knew the purchase price I was offering was too low. Not once had I given any thought about the interests of the seller. Not once had I even considered what would be fair to him. I had concentrated solely on acquiring the property at the lowest possible price.

I reexamined the transaction in the light of "looking intently" after the seller's interests as well as my own. After an intense inner struggle, I concluded that I should pay more for the property to reflect its true value. Practicing the Golden Rule is sometimes costly, but its reward is a clear conscience before God and other people.

THE FEAR OF THE LORD

When I talk of a "healthy fear" of the Lord, I do not mean that God is a big, celestial, club-wielding bully just waiting for the opportunity to punish us. He is rather a loving Father who, out of infinite love, disciplines His children for their benefit. *"He disciplines us for our good, that we may share His holiness"* (Hebrews 12:10).

One of the methods God uses to motivate us to honest living is this "healthy fear." Proverbs 16:6 reads, *"By the fear of the Lord one keeps away from evil."* Let me illustrate how the fear of the Lord helps us act honestly.

I once shared a motel room with a friend. As we were leaving, he slipped one of the motel's drinking glasses into his pocket and walked to the car. Suddenly I was overwhelmed by the fear of the Lord. It is difficult to explain the feeling. The closest description I've found is in Daniel 5:6, which records the Babylonian king's reaction to the handwriting on the wall: *"The king's thoughts troubled him, so that the joints of his loins were loosed, and his knees smote one against another"* (KJV).

There I was with my knees smiting each other! What came to mind was Hebrews 12:11, *"All discipline for the moment seems not to be joyful, but sorrowful."* Discipline hurts! Given the choice, I would much rather "share His holiness" out of obedience to His Word than to make a deliberate decision that would prompt my loving Father to discipline me. I was afraid for my friend and for myself as an accomplice.

LOSS OF PROPERTY

Moreover, I believe our heavenly Father will not allow us to keep anything we have acquired dishonestly. Proverbs 13:11 reads, *"Wealth obtained by fraud dwindles."*

During a class, a participant related that she had purchased four azalea plants but that the check-out clerk had only charged her for one. She knew it, but she left the store anyway without paying for the other three. She went on to say it was simply miraculous how quickly three of those azalea plants died—and the fourth wasn't doing too well, either! Think about this for a moment: If you become a parent and one of your children steals something, do you think you would allow the child to keep it? Of course not. You will demand that it be returned because the child's character would be destroyed if he kept stolen property. Not only would you insist upon its return, but you would also want the child to experience enough discomfort to produce a lasting impression. For instance, you might have the child ask forgiveness from the store manager. When our heavenly Father lovingly disciplines us, it is usually done in such a way that we will not forget. This can be painful or embarrassing.

You can imagine how relieved I was when my friend returned the motel's glass after he had been confronted!

ISOLATING OURSELVES FROM THE DISHONEST

Scripture teaches that we are deeply influenced by those around us, either for good or evil. David recognized this and said,

> *My eyes shall be upon the faithful of the land, that they may dwell with me; he who walks in a blameless way is the one who will minister to me. He who practices deceit shall not dwell within my house; he who speaks falsehood shall not maintain his position before me.*
>
> PSALM 101:6-7

> *"Wealth obtained by fraud dwindles."*
> (Proverbs 13:11)

Paul wrote, *"Do not be deceived: Bad company corrupts good morals"* (1 Corinthians 15:33). Solomon was even stronger: *"He who is a partner with a thief hates his own life"* (Proverbs 29:24).

Obviously, we cannot isolate ourselves from every dishonest person. In fact, we are to be salt and light in the world. We should, however, be very cautious with whom we associate, especially when considering a close relationship with someone.

It is much easier to remain absolutely honest if you are surrounded by others who are of a like mind and conviction. If I observe a person who is dishonest in his dealings with the government or in a small matter, I know this person will be dishonest in greater matters and probably in his dealings with me. In my opinion it is impossible for a person to be selectively honest. Either the person has made the commitment to be absolutely honest, or his relative honesty will become more prevalent.

> *It is much easier to remain absolutely honest if you are surrounded by others who are of a like mind and conviction.*

DEALING WITH DISHONESTY

Unfortunately, from time to time, we will act dishonestly, but once we recognize that we have, we need to do the following:

1. We must restore our fellowship with God. Anytime we sin we break our fellowship with our Lord. This needs to be restored as the first order of business. First John 1:9 tells us how: *"If we confess our sins, He is faithful and righteous to forgive us our sins and to cleanse us from all unrighteousness."*

We must agree with God that our dishonesty was sin and then thankfully accept God's gracious forgiveness so we can again enjoy His fellowship.

2. We must restore our fellowship with the offended person. After our fellowship with Christ has been restored, we need to confess our dishonesty to the person we offended. *"Confess your sins to one another"* (James 5:16).

Ouch! This hurts. I've had only a handful of people confess that they have wronged me. Interestingly, these are the very people who have become my closest friends, in part because of my respect for them. They so desired an honest relationship with me that they were willing to expose their sins.

This has been very hard for me. For the first time, several years ago I went to someone I had wronged and confessed my sin—not that I hadn't had plenty of opportunities before! In the past, however, my pride stood in the way. Afterward I sensed a great freedom in our relationship. I also discovered that, because it is a painfully humbling experience, confession helps break the habit of dishonesty.

A person's lack of financial prosperity may be a consequence of violating this principle.

He who conceals his transgressions will not prosper, but he
who confesses and forsakes them will find compassion.

PROVERBS 28:13

3. We must restore any dishonestly acquired property. If we
have acquired anything dishonestly, we must return it to its right-
ful owner.

Then it shall be, when he sins and becomes guilty that he
shall restore what he took by robbery . . . or anything about
which he swore falsely; he shall make restitution for it in full,
and add to it one-fifth more. He shall give it to the one to
whom it belongs.

LEVITICUS 6:4-5

Restitution is a tangible expression of repentance and an
effort to correct a wrong. Zaccheus is a good example. He
promised Jesus, *"If I have defrauded anyone of anything, I will give*
back four times as much" (Luke 19:8).

If it's not possible for restitution to be made to the injured
party, then the property should be given to the Lord. Numbers
5:8 teaches,

But if the man has no relative to whom restitution may be made for
the wrong, the restitution which is made for the wrong must go to the Lord
for the priest.

BRIBES

A bribe is defined as anything given to a person to influence
him to do something illegal or wrong. All too often we hear of
someone in business or politics who is arrested for bribery. The
taking of bribes is clearly prohibited in Scripture: *"And you shall*
not take a bribe, for a bribe blinds the clear-sighted and subverts the
cause of the just" (Exodus 23:8). Bribes are often subtly disguised
as a "gift" or "referral fee." Evaluate any such offer prayerfully
to confirm that it is not in reality a bribe.

> *Restitution is a tangible expression of repentance and an effort to correct a wrong.*

BLESSINGS AND CURSES

Listed below are some of the blessings the Lord has promised for
the honest and some of the curses reserved for the dishonest.
Read these slowly and prayerfully, asking God to use His Word
to motivate you to a life of honesty.

> ## BLESSINGS PROMISED FOR THE HONEST
>
> - Blessing of a more intimate relationship with the Lord: *"For the crooked man is an abomination to the Lord; but He is intimate with the upright"* (Proverbs 3:32).
> - Blessings on the family: *"A righteous man who walks in his integrity—how blessed are his sons after him"* (Proverbs 20:7).
> - Blessings of life: *"Truthful lips will be established forever, but a lying tongue is only for a moment"* (Proverbs 12:19).
> - Blessing of prosperity: *"Much wealth is in the house of the righteous, but trouble is in the income of the wicked"* (Proverbs 15:6).
>
> ## CURSES RESERVED FOR THE DISHONEST
>
> - Curse of alienation from God: *"For the crooked man is an abomination to the Lord"* (Proverbs 3:32).
> - Curse on the family: *"He who profits illicitly troubles his own house, but he who hates bribes will live"* (Proverbs 15:27).
> - Curse of death: *"The getting of treasures by a lying tongue is a fleeting vapor, the pursuit of death"* (Proverbs 21:6).
> - Curse of poverty: *"Wealth obtained by fraud dwindles"* (Proverbs 13:11).

PONDER YOUR FUTURE

All of us will serve in positions of leadership—either at school, in work, at church, or as a parent. The Lord is especially concerned with the honesty of leaders. Scripture addresses three areas of honesty in leadership:

INFLUENCE OF LEADERS

Leaders influence their subordinates. The owner of a trucking business began wearing cowboy boots to work. Within six months, all the men in his office were in boots. He suddenly changed to a traditional business shoe, and six months later all the men were wearing business shoes.

In a similar way, a dishonest leader produces dishonest followers. *"If a ruler pays attention to falsehood, all his ministers become wicked"* (Proverbs 29:12).

The president of a large international construction company was once asked why his company did not work in countries where bribes and graft were a way of life. He responded, "We never build in those countries, no matter how profitable the project may appear, because we can't afford to. If my employees know we are acting dishonestly, they will eventually become thieves. Their dishonesty will ultimately cost us more than we could ever earn on a project."

The leader must set the example of honesty in his or her personal life before those under their authority can be expected to do the same.

During an effort to reduce expenses, a company discovered the employees were making frequent, personal, long-distance telephone calls at the office and charging them to the company. The company president had unwittingly fueled this problem. He had reasoned that because he placed approximately the same number of company long-distance calls on his home phone as personal long-distance calls on the company phone, a detailed accounting and reimbursement were unnecessary.

But his employees knew only of his calls at work. They concluded that if this dishonest practice was acceptable for the boss, it was acceptable for all. A leader in particular should *"abstain from all appearance of evil"* (1 Thessalonians 5:22, KJV), because his or her actions influence others.

> *Scripture teaches that we are deeply influenced by those around us, either for good or evil.*

SELECTION OF LEADERS

Dishonesty should disqualify a person from leadership. Listen to the counsel of Jethro, Moses' father-in-law:

> *You shall select out of all the people able men who fear God, men of truth, those who hate dishonest gain; and you shall place these . . . as leaders of thousands, of hundreds, of fifties and of tens.*
>
> EXODUS 18:21

Two of the four criteria for leadership selection that Jethro gave Moses dealt with honesty — *"men of truth, those who hate dishonest gain."* I believe the Lord wants us to continue to select leaders on the basis of these same character qualities.

This is the big question for you to answer: Am I going to be committed to living an absolutely honest life that will please God and influence others? You will be tempted often to compromise. It will require courage.

If you want to make this commitment, there is no better place to start than right now while you are in school.

A Wise Person Seeks Advice

"The way of a fool is right in his own eyes, but a wise man is he who listens to counsel."

PROVERBS 12:15

MEMORIZE PROVERBS 12:15
"The way of a fool is right in his own eyes, but a wise man is he who listens to counsel."

PRACTICAL APPLICATION
Complete the Adjusting Your Budget practical application.

DAY ONE

Read Proverbs 12:15; Proverbs 13:10 and Proverbs 15:22 and answer:

What are some of the benefits of seeking counsel?

Proverbs 12:15 —

Proverbs 13:10 —

Proverbs 15:22 —

What are some of the benefits you have experienced from seeking counsel?

What hinders you from seeking counsel?

DAY TWO

Read Psalm 16:7 and Psalm 32:8 and answer:

Does the Lord actively counsel his children?

Then read Psalm 106:13-15.

In this passage what was the consequence of not seeking the Lord's counsel?

Have you ever suffered for not seeking the Lord's counsel? If so, describe what happened.

How do you personally seek the Lord's counsel?

DAY THREE

Read Psalm 119:24; Psalm 119:105; 2 Timothy 3:16-17 and Hebrews 4:12.

Why should the Bible also serve as your counselor?

Then read *Psalm 119:98-100*. Living by the counsel of Scripture will:

Do you read and study the Bible as consistently as you should? If not, what prevents your consistency?

DAY FOUR

Read Proverbs 1:8-9.

Who should be among your counselors?

Do you actively seek counsel from your parents? If not, why?

Read Proverbs 11:14 and Ecclesiastes 4:9-12.

What do these verses communicate to you?

Proverbs 11:14—

Ecclesiastes 4:9-12—

How do you propose to apply this principle?

Read Psalm 1:1-3 and answer:

Whom should you avoid as a counselor?

What is your definition of a wicked person?

Is there ever a circumstance in which you should seek the input of a person who does not know Christ? If so, when?

DAY FIVE

Read the *Counsel Notes* and answer:

What in the notes particularly interested you?

What issues are you currently facing that require wise counsel?

Whom will you ask for advice concerning these issues?

DAY SIX
PONDER YOUR FUTURE

Who do you think should be the number one counselor of a husband? Of a wife? Why?

My prayer request for the coming week:

COUNSEL NOTES

I frequently counsel people who have financial problems. Some of these people have lost literally millions of dollars and have subjected themselves to years of heartache and stress. More often than not, they could have avoided these difficulties if they had sought a few minutes of counsel from someone with a solid understanding of God's perspective of money.

SEEKING COUNSEL

People often avoid seeking counsel because of three common attitudes, the first of which is *pride*. Our culture perceives seeking advice as a sign of weakness. We are told, "Stand on your own two feet. You don't need anyone to help make your decisions for you!"

College is one of the most exciting and challenging times of life. Often with it comes a great deal of newly found independence. Being on your own is wonderful. However, mix this freedom with some youthful pride, and you might soon begin to think, "I'm on my own now, and nobody tells me what to do!"

Willful stubbornness, the second attitude, is characterized by the statement, "Don't confuse me with the facts. My mind is already made up!" People often resist seeking counsel because they do not want to be confronted with the facts another person might discover. We don't want to be told we can't afford that beautiful new car we have already decided to buy.

The *generation gap* is the third hindrance to seeking counsel. An older person might reject a progressive idea advanced by a college student because of his inexperience. A student might disregard advice from an elder counselor because it comes from someone "old." As hard as it may be for some students to believe, older, experienced counselors are among their most valuable sources of good advice.

A story in 1 Kings 12 illustrates this. When Rehoboam inherited the kingdom of Israel from his father Solomon, his subjects asked the new king to reduce their taxes in return for their continued loyalty. Rehoboam first consulted with the elders who advised him to comply with their request. However, *"He forsook the counsel of the elders which they had given him, and consulted with the young men who grew up with him"* (1 Kings 12:8). His young friends rashly advised the king to respond harshly and raise taxes. Rehoboam followed their advice and promptly lost the majority of his kingdom.

The admonition from God's Word is in stark contrast to the practice of making decisions without counsel. Proverbs 19:20 reads, *"Listen to advice and accept instruction, and in the end you will be wise"* (NIV). And Proverbs 12:15 says, *"The way of a fool is right in his own eyes, but a wise man is he who listens to counsel."* I like Proverbs 10:8 from the Living Bible: *"The wise man is glad to be instructed, but a self-sufficient fool falls flat on his face."*

One seeks counsel to secure insights, suggestions and alternatives that will aid in making a proper decision. It is not the counselor's role to make the decision. You retain that responsibility.

"Dear Lord, let me be the big cheese in the number-one job of the top outfit in the country, and let me come up with the right answers at the right times in the right places, but with it all, let me remain soft-spoken, country-shy, plain old Jeff Crotts from Spickard, Missouri."

©1988 Henry R. Martin. Reprinted with permission.

BEYOND THE FACTS

We need to assemble the facts that will influence our decision, but we should not base our decision exclusively upon those facts. We must determine specifically what the Lord wants us to do, and this may be contrary to what the facts alone would dictate.

The importance of going beyond simply collecting the facts is clearly illustrated in Numbers chapters 13 and 14. Moses sent twelve spies into the Promised Land. All of the spies returned with an identical assessment of the facts. It was a prosperous land flowing with milk and honey, but one, however, that was occupied by terrifying giants. They were all technically correct. But only two of the twelve spies, Joshua and Caleb, went beyond the facts. They knew what the Lord wanted them to do. Irrespective of the obstacles, He was going to miraculously enable them to possess the Promised Land.

The children of Israel relied only upon the tangible facts and did not act in faith upon what the Lord wanted for them. Consequently, they suffered forty years of wandering in the wilderness and the death of a generation.

SOURCES OF COUNSEL

What are the sources of counsel we need to seek? Before I make a financial decision, particularly an important one, I subject the decision to three sources of counsel.

THE COUNSEL OF SCRIPTURE

First of all, what does God's Word say about a particular issue? The psalmist wrote, *"Your laws are both my light and my counselors"* (Psalm 119:24, LB). Psalm 119:98-100 reads,

> *Thy commandments make me wiser than my enemies, for they are ever mine. I have more insight than all my teachers, for Thy testimonies are my meditation. I understand more than the aged, because I have observed Thy precepts.*

The Bible tells us that by searching the Scriptures we can have more insight and more wisdom than those who, without the knowledge of God's Word, are educated and experienced in the ways of our culture. I would always rather obey the truth of Scripture than risk suffering the financial consequences of following my own inclinations or the opinions of people who don't have a biblical perspective.

The Bible makes this remarkable claim about itself: *"For the word of God is living and active and sharper than any two edged sword . . . and . . . able to judge the thoughts and intentions of the heart"* (Hebrews 4:12). The Bible is a living book that our Lord uses to communicate His truths that are relevant for all generations.

It may have come as a surprise to you to learn that Scripture contains 2,350 verses dealing with how we should handle money. The very first filter I put a financial decision through is Scripture. If God's Word clearly answers my question, I do not have to seek any further because the Bible contains the Lord's written, revealed will.

Bob and Barbara were faced with a difficult decision. Barbara's brother and his wife had just moved to Florida from Chicago. Because they experienced financial difficulties in Chicago, the bank would not lend them the money to purchase a home unless they had someone cosign the note. They asked Bob and Barbara to cosign.

Bob was reluctant, even though Barbara pleaded for him to do so. A friend referred them to the verses that warn against cosigning. After Barbara read the passages she responded, "Well, who am I to argue with God? We shouldn't cosign." Bob was tremendously relieved.

Two years later, Barbara's brother and his wife were divorced, and her brother declared bankruptcy. If Bob had cosigned that note, they probably would not have been able to survive financially. Can you imagine the strain that decision would have put on their marriage?

If the Bible tells us to do something, do it. If the Bible tells us not to do something, don't do it. If the Bible is not specific about a particular issue, subject your decision to the second source of counsel—godly people.

> *The Bible is a living book that our Lord uses to communicate his direction and truths, which are relevant for all generations.*

THE COUNSEL OF GODLY PEOPLE

"The godly man is a good counselor, because he is just and fair and knows right from wrong" (Psalm 37:30-31, LB). The Christian life is not one of independence from other Christians but of dependence upon one other. In Paul's discussion concerning the body of Christ in 1 Corinthians 12, individuals are likened to various members of the body—the eyes, the ears, the hands. Our ability to function properly is dependent upon the members working together. God has given each of us certain abilities and gifts, but God has not given any one person all the abilities that he or she needs to be most productive.

So when facing important decisions, we need to seek the advice of men and women who are gifted to give us wise and godly counsel.

OUR PARENTS

A wonderful source of counsel is our parents. Proverbs 6:20-22 says:

> *My son, observe the commandment of your father, and do not forsake the teaching of your mother; bind them continually on your heart; tie them around your neck. When you walk about, they will guide you; when you sleep, they will watch over you; and when you awake, they will talk to you.*

I cannot tell you how much I have benefited from the counsel of my father and mother. Our parents have the benefit of years of experience, they know us so very well, and they have our best interest at heart.

In my opinion we should seek their counsel even if they do not yet know Christ or have not been faithful money managers themselves. Barriers often grow up between children and parents over the years. It is a compliment for anyone to be asked for advice—an expression of admiration. Asking advice from parents is a way of honoring them.

EXPERIENCED PEOPLE

We should also consult people experienced in the area in which we are attempting to make a decision. If I am going to purchase a car, I will locate a trustworthy automobile mechanic and ask him to examine the car and give me his opinion before I complete the purchase. If I need to refine my financial situation, I will seek a wise financial advisor.

A MULTITUDE OF COUNSELORS

Proverbs 15:22 reads, *"Without consultation, plans are frustrated, but with many counselors they succeed."* And Proverbs 11:14 says,

"Now remember, John, no honey until you've finished all your locusts."

"*Where there is no guidance, the people fall, but in abundance of counselors there is victory.*" Each of us has a limited range of knowledge and experience. We need the insight and input of others who bring their own unique backgrounds to broaden our thinking with alternatives we would never have considered without their advice.

GROW UP...QUIT WHINING...GET OUTTA HERE.

I meet regularly with a group to pray and share our lives together. The members of our group know each other well. Over the years all of us have been confronted with difficult circumstances or major decisions. We have observed that when someone is subjected to a painful circumstance, it is very difficult to make wise, dispassionate decisions. We have experienced the benefits and safety of having a group of people who love one another, who know one another, and who can give prayerful, objective counsel to one another—even when it hurts. I am more receptive to constructive criticism when it comes from someone I respect and who I know cares for me.

Solomon describes the benefits of dependence upon one another:

> *Two are better than one because they have a good return for their labor. For if either of them falls, the one will lift up his companion. But woe to the one who falls when there is not another to lift him up. Furthermore, if two lie down together they keep warm, but how can one be warm alone? And if one can overpower him who is alone, two can resist him. A cord of three strands is not quickly torn apart.*
>
> ECCLESIASTES 4:9-12

It can be very productive to gather your counselors together. Frequently the suggestions of one will stimulate insights from another. What one says can be confirmed, disputed, or discussed by the others. It is not uncommon for a clear direction or unanimous conclusion to be established when all of your counselors gather together.

When seeking a multitude of counselors, they often will not offer the same recommendations; in fact, there can be sharp disagreement. But usually a common thread will begin to develop. Sometimes each counselor will supply you with a different piece of the puzzle that you need to make the decision.

THE COUNSEL OF THE LORD

During the process of analyzing the facts, searching the Bible and obtaining the counsel of many godly people, we need to be seeking direction from the Lord. In Isaiah 9:6 we are told

Each of us has a limited range of knowledge and experience; we need the input of others, who bring their own unique backgrounds to give us insight and stimulate our thinking with alternatives we would never have considered without their advice.

that one of the Lord's names is *"Wonderful Counselor."*

The Psalms clearly identify the Lord as our counselor. *"I [the Lord] will instruct you and teach you in the way which you should go; I will counsel you with My eye upon you"* (Psalm 32:8). *"You [the Lord] guide me with your counsel"* (Psalm 73:24, NIV). *"I will bless the Lord who has counseled me"* (Psalm 16:7).

In Scripture there are numerous examples of the unfortunate consequences of not seeking God's counsel, as well as the blessings of heeding His counsel. After the children of Israel began their successful campaign to capture the Promised Land, some of the natives (Gibeonites) attempted to enter into a peace treaty with Israel. The Gibeonites deceived the leaders of Israel into believing they were from a distant land.

> *So the men of Israel took some of their [Gibeonites] provisions and did not ask for the counsel of the Lord. And Joshua made peace with them and made a covenant with them, to let them live.*
>
> JOSHUA 9:14-15

The consequence of Israel not seeking the Lord's counsel was that the Promised Land remained populated with ungodly people, and Israel was eventually ensnared by their false gods. The leaders were influenced by the "facts" they could see — facts that were designed to deceive the leaders into thinking that the Gibeonites were not natives living in the Promised Land. Often only the Lord can reveal to us real truth and proper direction. Only the Lord knows the future and the ultimate consequences of a decision.

THE IMPORTANCE OF BEING QUIET

Our culture has been described as one of busyness, entertainment, crowds and noise. Throughout Scripture, however, we are admonished to wait upon the Lord. When we are undistracted by activity, focused on the Lord, we can understand most clearly what He is telling us. It is more than coincidence that many of the godliest characters in Scripture spent time in quiet isolation — Moses 40 years in the desert, David tending flocks, Paul in prison, and Jesus Himself 40 days in the desert. Whenever you feel hurried or pressured, or you experience a sense of confusion concerning a decision, discipline yourself to go to a quiet place. Listen prayerfully and quietly for His still, small voice. The world around you screams, "Hurry!," but the Lord tells you to wait.

Only the Lord knows the future and the ultimate consequences of a decision.

COUNSEL OF THE WICKED

We need to avoid one particular source of counsel. *"How blessed is the man who does not walk in the counsel of the wicked"* (Psalm 1:1). The word "blessed" literally means to be "happy many times over." The definition of a "wicked" person is one who lives his life without regard to God. A wicked person can either be a person who does not yet personally know the Lord, or one who knows Jesus Christ as Savior but is not following Him in obedience. Avoid such counsel like the plague.

In my opinion, when you are searching for facts or technical information, you may seek input from those who do not know Christ. But gathering information and seeking counsel are two different things. Seek counsel only from those with godly values and perspectives.

FORTUNE-TELLERS, MEDIUMS, OR SPIRITUALISTS

The Bible bluntly tells us never to seek the advice of fortune-tellers, mediums, or spiritualists: *"Do not turn to mediums or spiritists; do not seek them out to be defiled by them. I am the Lord your God"* (Leviticus 19:31). Study this next passage carefully:

> *So Saul died for his trespass which he committed against the Lord . . . and also because he asked counsel of a medium, making inquiry of it, and did not inquire of the Lord. Therefore He killed him.*
>
> 1 CHRONICLES 10:13-14

Saul died, in part, because he went to a medium. We should also avoid any methods they use in forecasting the future, such as horoscopes and all other practices of the occult.

BIASED COUNSELORS

A wise person considers factors that may influence someone's counsel. If you ask a computer salesman if he thinks you need a new computer, what do you think he is inclined to say? "Of course you need a new computer."

We need to be cautious of the counsel of the biased. When receiving financial advice, ask yourself this question: "What stake does this person have in the outcome of my decision? Does he stand to gain or lose from this decision?" If the advisor will profit, be cautious when evaluating his counsel and always seek a second unbiased opinion.

A FINAL WORD

When you are seeking advice, supply your counselor with all the important facts. Do not attempt to manipulate your advisor to give the answer you want to hear by concealing pertinent information.

Whenever you are faced with a major financial decision such as a career direction or whether to attend graduate school, it is helpful to go to a secluded place where you can spend uninterrupted time prayerfully reading Scripture and seeking the Lord. I encourage you to consider fasting during this time.

Be selective in choosing your counselors. Make sure they have the courage to give you advice that may be contrary to your wishes. Always attempt to include those who are gifted with wisdom. *"He who walks with wise men will be wise"* (Proverbs 13:20). Continually ask the Lord for wisdom.

> *But if any of you lacks wisdom, let him ask of God, who gives to all men generously and without reproach, and it will be given to him. But let him ask in faith without any doubting.*
>
> JAMES 1:5-6

As you seek counsel, do not be surprised if the answer comes out of your own mouth. Interacting with others allows you the opportunity to verbalize thoughts and feelings that you may have never before expressed clearly.

PONDER YOUR FUTURE

During college and in the years that immediately follow, many decisions are made that affect the rest of your life. The big ones are curriculum, career and marriage.

CURRICULUM AND CAREER

Many colleges require freshmen to declare a major at the very beginning. In addition to this, the number of required core courses is decreasing at many schools. Consequently, students must make decisions earlier on the areas in which they will major. As you work through curriculum and career options, it is important to seek out people in the fields you are considering. Think carefully about the questions you need to ask them. You should find out how they decided on their own careers. What do they like most about their jobs? What do they like the least?

John McCutchen was a student in medical school and was training to become a heart surgeon. He had a long conversation with the chief heart surgeon in the medical school and discovered he was not suited for the lifestyle, which included the stress of emergency operations, long and unpredictable hours and serving patients who were dying. Instead, he became an outstanding orthopedic surgeon who has specialized in hip replacement. Emergencies are rare, and he is able to spend more consistent time with his family.

Very few jobs are exactly what they seem to be. Do not make big decisions based on assumptions until you have done some research and know for sure.

Marriage

If you are not married but you sense this is what God may want for you, let me encourage you to consistently pray for the Lord, in His time, to bring a godly person into your life as a spouse. After 27 years of marriage I can tell you there are few things more precious than a godly spouse.

If you marry, the first person you need to consult is your spouse. Frankly, it has been a humbling experience for me to seek the counsel of my wife, Bev, in financial matters. I was in business for many years, and she has no formal financial training. Nevertheless, she has saved me a great deal of money by her wise counsel.

I am occasionally exposed to investment opportunities. A slick salesman will tell me how I can make an investment that will put us on easy street. I'll get excited and tell Bev about this terrific new investment. She will sit quietly and listen. Then she will often say, "Howard, that sounds wonderful, but I just don't feel good about it."

Women tend to be gifted with a wonderfully sensitive and intuitive nature that is usually very accurate. Men tend to focus objectively on the facts. Husbands and wives need each other to achieve the proper balance for a correct decision. I also believe that the Lord honors the wife's "office" or "position" as helpmate to her husband. Many times the Lord communicates most clearly to the husband through his wife.

OXYMORONS ILLUSTRATED

Male Intellect

To those of you who will become husbands, let me be blunt. Regardless of her business background or her financial aptitude, you must cultivate and seek your wife's counsel. I have committed never to proceed with a financial decision in excess of $100 unless Bev agrees. There are additional benefits from seeking your spouse's counsel:

1. It will preserve your relationship! The husband and wife should agree, because they will both experience the consequences of the decision. Even if their choice proves to be disastrous, their relationship remains intact. There are no grounds for an "I told you so" response.

2. It will honor your wife and prepare her for the future. When a husband seeks his wife's advice, he is actually communicating, "I love you. I respect you. I value your insight." Consistently asking for her advice also keeps your wife informed of your true financial condition. This is important in the event you predecease her or are unable to work. My father suffered a massive heart attack that incapacitated him for two years. Because he had been faithful in keeping my mother abreast of his business, she was able to step in and operate the business successfully until he recovered.

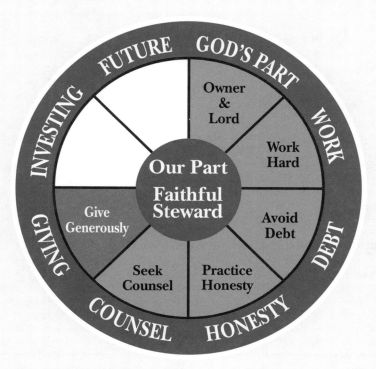

Giving Is Blessed—

"Remember the words of the Lord Jesus,
that He Himself said, 'It is more blessed
to give than to receive.'"

ACTS 20:35

MEMORIZE
ACTS 20:35
"Remember the words of
the Lord Jesus, that He
Himself said, 'It is more
blessed to give than to
receive.'"

PRACTICAL
APPLICATION
Complete the Beginning
Your Budget practical
application.

DAY ONE

Read 1 Corinthians 13:3 and 2 Corinthians 9:7 and answer:

What do these passages communicate about the importance of the proper attitude in giving?

1 Corinthians 13:3—

2 Corinthians 9:7—

How do you think a person can develop the proper attitude in giving?

After prayerfully evaluating your attitude in giving, how would you describe it?

DAY TWO

Read Acts 20:35 and answer:

How does this principle from God's economy differ from the way most people view giving?

List the benefits for the giver, which are found in each of the following passages:

Proverbs 11:24-25—

Matthew 6:20—

Luke 12:34—

1 Timothy 6:18-19—

DAY THREE

Read Malachi 3:8-10.

Was the tithe required under Old Testament Law?

Then read 2 Corinthians 8:1-5.

Identify three principles from this passage that should influence how much you give.

    1.

    2.

    3.

Prayerfully seek the Lord's guidance to determine how much you should give. You will not be asked to disclose the amount.

Read 1 Timothy 5:8 and answer:

Does the Bible require us to take care of our family members? How does this apply to you?

Then read Galatians 6:6 and 1 Timothy 5:17-18.

What do these verses tell you about financially supporting your church and those who teach the Scriptures?

Galatians 6:6 —

1 Timothy 5:17-18 —

DAY FOUR _____

Read Isaiah 58:6-11 and Ezekiel 16:49 and answer:

What do these verses say about giving to the poor?

Isaiah 58:6-11 —

Ezekiel 16:49 —

Then study Matthew 25:35-45.

How does Jesus Christ identify with the poor?

Then read Galatians 2:9-10.

What does this verse communicate to you about giving to the poor?

Are you currently giving to the poor? If not, what is hindering you?

DAY FIVE_____

Read the *Giving Notes* and answer:

How will your recognition of the importance of giving with the proper attitude impact your giving?

What did you learn about giving that proved especially interesting? In what way?

DAY SIX
PONDER YOUR FUTURE_____

Write your "autobiography of giving" by describing your attitude toward giving, how much you have given and who you have given to.

Now take time and pray. Ask the Lord to give you His vision for your future giving. Describe your sense of what the Lord wants your giving to be in the future.

My prayer request for the coming week:

GIVING NOTES

Few areas of the Christian life can be more frustrating than that of giving. For several years after I met Christ, I struggled with the whole concept of giving and would go to almost any length to avoid it. On a few occasions I found myself in a position in which I felt obligated to give in order to keep up spiritual appearances. I did so, but my heart wasn't really in it.

My whole perspective changed once I learned what Scripture actually taught. I then had a newly found desire to give, but I was frustrated by another problem: an unlimited number of needs and my limited resources. How could I decide to whom I should give? My local church, the hungry poor, campus ministries and prison outreaches, missionary efforts, Christian broadcasting and many other vital ministries all needed financial support.

We will examine the four elements having to do with giving: attitudes, advantages, amount and approach.

ATTITUDES IN GIVING

God's attitude about giving is best summed up in John 3:16: *"For God so loved the world, that He gave His only begotten Son."* Note the sequence: God gave because He loved. By sending His Son to die on the cross for us, He set the example of giving motivated by love.

The apostle Paul wrote: *"If I give all my possessions to feed the poor . . . but do not have love, it profits me nothing"* (1 Corinthians 13:3). It is hard to imagine anything more commendable than giving everything to the poor. But giving with a wrong attitude, without being motivated by love, is of no benefit to the giver.

In God's economy our attitude is infinitely more important than the amount. The spirit is more important than the sum. In fact, God evaluates our actions on the basis of our attitudes.

The Pharisees were fanatically precise about giving. They would calculate the tithe right down to the last mint leaf in their gardens. God, however, looks past the amount

In God's economy our attitude is infinitely more important than the amount.

of the gift to the heart of the giver. Christ rebuked them for their wrong attitude, saying:

Woe to you, scribes and Pharisees, hypocrites! For you tithe mint and dill and cummin, and have neglected the weightier provisions of the law: justice and mercy and faithfulness; but these are the things you should have done without neglecting the others.

MATTHEW 23:23

"That was the best sermon on giving I've ever heard."

For giving to be of any value, it must be done from a heart of love.

Our basis for giving out of a heart filled with love is the recognition that even though our gifts are given through the agency of people and for their benefit, they are actually given to the Lord Himself. An example of this is found in Numbers 18:24: *"For the tithe of the sons of Israel, which they offer as an offering to the Lord, I have given to the Levites for an inheritance."* If giving is merely to a church, a ministry, or a needy person, it is only charity. But if gifts are given to the Lord, they become acts of worship. We have the privilege of expressing our gratefulness and love by giving gifts to our Creator, our Savior and our faithful Provider. When the offering plate is being passed at church, we should consciously remind ourselves that we are giving our gift to the Lord Himself.

In addition to giving out of a heart filled with love, we are to give cheerfully.

Let each one do just as he has purposed in his heart; not grudgingly or under compulsion; for God loves a cheerful giver.
2 CORINTHIANS 9:7

The original Greek word translated here "cheerful" is *hilaros,* from which the English word "hilarious" is derived. We are to be hilarious givers, beside ourselves with glee over the prospect of giving to Christ Himself.

There is usually little hilarity in the pews when the offering plate is passed at church. In fact, the atmosphere often is reminiscent of a patient waiting in the dentist's chair knowing a painful extraction is about to occur.

How do we develop this hilarity in our giving? Consider the early churches of Macedonia.

Now, brethren, we wish to make known to you the grace of God which has been given in the churches of Macedonia, that in a great ordeal of affliction their abundance of joy and their deep poverty overflowed in the wealth of their liberality.
2 CORINTHIANS 8:1-2

Reprinted from *Off the Church Wall* by Rob Portlock. ©1987 by Rob Portlock. Used by permission of Intervarsity Press. P.O. Box 1400 Downers Grove, IL 60515

How did the Macedonians, who were in terrible circumstances, *"great affliction and deep poverty,"* still manage to give with an *"abundance of joy"*? The answer is in verse 5: *"They first gave themselves to the Lord and to us by the will of God."* Cheerful giving begins by submitting yourself to Christ. Ask Him to direct how much He wants you to give. Only then are we in a position to reap any of the advantages by giving with the proper attitude.

Stop and examine yourself. What is your attitude toward giving?

ADVANTAGES OF GIVING

It is easy to understand how a gift benefits the recipient. The local church continues its ministry, the hungry are fed, the naked are clothed and missionaries are sent. But according to God's economy, a gift given with the proper attitude benefits the giver more than the receiver. *"Remember the words of the Lord Jesus, that He Himself said, 'It is more blessed to give than to receive'"* (Acts 20:35). As we examine Scripture, we find that the giver benefits in four significant areas:

AN INCREASE IN INTIMACY
Above all else, giving directs our attentions and hearts to Christ. Matthew 6:21 tells us, *"For where your treasure is, there will your heart be also."* This is why it is so necessary to consciously give each gift to the person of Jesus Christ. When you give your gift to Him, your heart will automatically be drawn to the Lord.

AN INCREASE IN CHARACTER
Our heavenly Father wants us as His children to be conformed to the image of His Son. While humans are by nature selfish, the character of Christ is that of an unselfish giver. By habitually

"Let each one do just as he has purposed in his heart; not grudgingly or under compulsion; for God loves a cheerful giver." (2 Corinthians 9:7)

giving, we are continually being conformed to Christ. Someone once said, "Giving is not God's way of raising money; it is God's way of raising people into the likeness of His Son."

AN INCREASE IN HEAVEN

The Lord tells us that there really is something akin to the "First National Bank of Heaven." And He wants us to know that we can invest for eternity.

> *But lay up for yourselves treasures in heaven, where neither moth nor rust destroys, and where thieves do not break in and steal.*
>
> MATTHEW 6:20

Paul also wrote, *"Not that I seek the gift itself, but I seek for the profit which increases to your account"* (Philippians 4:17). There is an account for each of us in heaven which we will be privileged to enjoy for eternity. And while it is true that we "can't take it with us," Scripture teaches that we can make deposits to our heavenly account before we die.

AN INCREASE ON EARTH

Some people react to those who teach what I call "giving to get." You may have heard some assert that if you give, God will repay you one-hundred fold and you will become rich! Many people have a hard time believing that, beyond the spiritual blessings, giving actually results in material blessings flowing back to the giver. But study the passages below.

The Saturday Evening Post.

"**What's this we hear about you laying up treasures in heaven?**"

> *There is one who scatters, yet increases all the more, and there is one who withholds what is justly due, but it results only in want. The generous man will be prosperous, and he who waters will himself be watered.*
>
> PROVERBS 11:24-25

> *Now this I say, he who sows sparingly shall also reap sparingly; and he who sows bountifully shall also reap bountifully . . . God is able to make all grace abound to you, that always having all sufficiency in everything, you may have an abundance for every good deed; as it is written, "He*

scattered abroad, He gave to the poor, His righteousness abides forever." Now He who supplies seed to the sower and bread for food, will supply and multiply your seed for sowing and increase the harvest of your righteousness; you will be enriched in everything for all liberality.

2 CORINTHIANS 9:6-11

These verses clearly teach that giving does result in a material increase. Those who give "*shall also reap bountifully . . . always having all sufficiency in everything . . . may have an abundance . . . will supply and multiply your seed . . . you will be enriched in everything.*" But note carefully **why** the Lord is returning an increase materially: "*Always having all sufficiency in everything, you may have an abundance for every good deed . . . will supply and multiply your seed for sowing . . . you will be enriched in everything for all liberality.*" As shown in the diagram to the right, the Lord produces a material increase so that we may give more and have our needs met at the same time.

One reason the Lord reveals that a gift will result in material increase is that He wants us to recognize He is sovereignly behind the multiplication of our seed. God has chosen to be invisible, but He wants us to experience His reality. When we give, we should do so with a sense of expectancy—anticipating the Lord to provide a material increase, even though we do not know when or how the Lord will choose to provide this increase. From my experiences, I know He can be very creative!

The giver can reap the advantages of giving only when he gives cheerfully out of a heart filled with love, not when the motive of giving is just to get.

AMOUNT TO GIVE

Let's survey what the Scriptures say about how much to give. Under Old Testament law a tithe (literally, a tenth) was required. The Lord condemns the children of Israel in the Book of Malachi for not tithing properly:

Will a man rob God? Yet you are robbing Me! But you say, "How have we robbed Thee?" In tithes and offerings. You are cursed with a curse, for you are robbing Me, the whole nation of you!

MALACHI 3:8-9

In addition to the tithe, there were various compulsory and free-will offerings. The Lord also made special provision for the needs of the poor. Every seven years all debts were forgiven, every fifty years the land was returned to the original land-owning families, and special rules allowed the poor to glean behind the harvesters and along the edges of the fields.

In the New Testament the tithe is neither specifically rejected nor specifically recommended. What is clearly taught is that we are to give in proportion to the material blessing we have received. The New Testament also commends sacrificial giving.

What I like about the tithe or any fixed percentage of giving is that it is systematic, and the amount of the gift is easy to compute. On the other hand, the danger of the tithe is that it can be treated as simply another bill to be paid. Tithing with a wrong attitude does not put me in a position to receive the blessings and advantages God has for me. Another potential danger of tithing is the assumption that once the tithe is given, all my obligations to contribute are fulfilled. For many Christians the tithe should be the beginning of their giving, not the limit. In my family we are convinced that we should tithe as a minimum and then give over and above the tithe as the Lord prospers and/or directs us.

APPROACH TO GIVING

One of the priorities of Paul's third missionary journey was to take up a collection for the suffering believers in Jerusalem. His advice to the Christians at Corinth was:

> *On the first day of every week let each one of you put aside and save, as he may prosper, that no collections be made when I come.*
>
> 1 CORINTHIANS 16:2

There are several practical principles contained in Paul's instructions to the Corinthians concerning this collection.

1. Giving should be periodic. *"On the first day of every week . . ."* The Lord understands that we need to give frequently and habitually. Giving only once a year, as some do, is a mistake. We need to give regularly, because we need to be drawn consistently to Christ.

2. Giving should be personal. *"Let each one of you . . ."* It is both the responsibility and the privilege of every child of God to give. If you are not yet consistently giving, now is a choice time. While you are a college student adopt this godly habit. The advantages of giving are intended for each person, and to be enjoyed, each individual must participate.

3. Giving should be out of a private deposit. *"Put aside and save . . ."* Many people have difficulty keeping track of the money they have decided to give. Consider opening a separate checking account (we call ours the "Lord's Account") or setting aside a special "cookie jar" into which you deposit the money you intend to give. Then as needs are brought to your attention, you will already have the money set aside to meet those needs.

4. Giving should be a priority. *"Honor the Lord from your wealth, and from the first of all your produce"* (Proverbs 3:9). As soon as we receive any income we should set aside the amount we are going to give. This habit helps us to remember to put Christ first in all we do and defeats the temptation to spend on ourselves the portion we have decided to give.

5. Giving should be premeditated. *"Let each one do just as he has purposed in his heart"* (2 Corinthians 9:7). Our giving should be done prayerfully, exercising the same care in selecting where we are going to give our money as we do when deciding where to invest our money.

6. Giving should be without pride. To experience any of the Lord's benefits, your giving cannot be motivated out of a desire to impress people.

Beware of practicing your righteousness before men to be noticed by them; otherwise you have no reward with your Father who is in heaven. When therefore you give alms, do not sound a trumpet before you, as the hypocrites do in the synagogues and in the streets, that they may be honored by men. Truly I say to you, they have their reward in full. But when you give alms, do not let your left hand know what your right hand is doing that your alms may be in secret; and your Father who sees in secret will repay you.

MATTHEW 6:1-4

PLACES FOR GIVING

We are instructed in Scripture to give to three areas. To whom and in what proportion one gives varies with the needs God lays on the heart of each believer.

GIVING TO THE LOCAL CHURCH AND CHRISTIAN MINISTRIES

Throughout its pages the Bible focuses on maintenance of the ministry. The Old Testament priesthood was to receive specific support: *"And to the sons of Levi, behold, I have given all the tithe in Israel . . . in return for their service which they perform, the service of the tent of meeting"* (Numbers 18:21). The New Testament teaching on ministerial support is just as strong. Unfortunately some have wrongly taught that those who are in various forms of Christian ministry should be poor. That position is not scriptural.

Pastors who do their work well should be paid well and should be highly appreciated, especially those who work hard at both preaching and teaching.

1 TIMOTHY 5:17, LB

People ask Bev and me if we give only to our church. In our case, the answer is no. However, we do give a minimum of ten percent of our regular income to our church because we believe this is a tangible expression of our commitment to our church. But we also give to others who are directly impacting us.

And let the one who is taught the word share all good things with him who teaches.

GALATIANS 6:6

GIVING TO THE FAMILY

In our culture we are experiencing a tragic breakdown in this area of giving. Husbands have failed to provide for their wives; parents have neglected their children; and grown sons and daughters have forsaken their elderly parents. Such neglect is solemnly condemned.

If anyone does not provide for his own, and especially for those of his household, he has denied the faith, and is worse than an unbeliever.

1 TIMOTHY 5:8

Meeting the needs of your family and relatives is a priority in giving and one in which there should be no compromise.

GIVING TO THE POOR

In Matthew 25 we are confronted with one of the most exciting and yet sobering truths in Scripture. Read this passage carefully:

Then the King will say ". . . For I was hungry and you gave Me something to eat; I was thirsty, and you gave Me drink." Then the righteous will answer Him, saying, "Lord, when did we see You hungry, and feed You, or thirsty, and give You drink?" . . . The King will answer and say to them, "Truly I say to you, to the extent that you did it to one of these brothers of Mine, even the least of them, you did it to Me." Then He will say to those on His left, "Depart from Me, accursed ones, into the eternal fire . . . For I was hungry, and you gave Me nothing to eat; I was thirsty, and you gave Me nothing to drink . . . to the extent that you did not do it to one of the least of these, you did not do it to Me."

MATTHEW 25:34-45

Used by permission of Rob Portlock

"Hi, Pastor. We were just talking about your request for a salary increase."

In some mysterious way we cannot fully comprehend, Jesus, the Creator of all things, personally identifies Himself with the poor. When we share with the poor, we are actually sharing with Jesus Himself. And if that truth is staggering, then the reciprocal is terrifying—when we do not give to the poor, we leave Christ Himself hungry and thirsty.

During Christ's earthly ministry He gave consistently to the poor. It is especially revealing that during the Last Supper, after Jesus told Judas to go and carry out the betrayal, this comment is made:

> *Now no one of those reclining at table knew for what purpose He had said this to him. For some were supposing, because Judas had the money box, that Jesus was saying to him, "Buy things we have need of for the feast;" or else, that he should give something to the poor.*
>
> JOHN 13:28-29

Giving to the poor was such a consistent part of Jesus' life that the disciples assumed that Jesus was sending Judas either to buy food for their own basic needs or to give to the poor—no other alternative entered their minds. It is no wonder that when Paul meets with the disciples to announce his call as a minister to the Gentiles, the disciples affirm his call with this stipulation: *"They* [the disciples] *only asked us to remember the poor—the very thing I also was eager to do"* (Galatians 2:10).

Imagine all the theological issues the disciples could have discussed with Paul, but the only one they mentioned was to remember the poor. Now that should tell us something!

Three areas of our Christian life are affected by giving or lack of giving to the poor:

> *Jesus, the Creator of all things, personally identifies himself with the poor.*

1. A LACK OF GIVING TO THE POOR COULD BE A SOURCE OF UNANSWERED PRAYER.

> *Is this not the fast which I chose . . . divide your bread with the hungry, and bring the homeless poor into the house . . . then you will call and the Lord will answer.*
>
> ISAIAH 58:6-9

> *He who shuts his ear to the cry of the poor will also cry himself and not be answered.*
>
> PROVERBS 21:13

2. OUR PROVISION IS CONDITIONED UPON OUR GIVING TO THE NEEDY.

He who gives to the poor will never want, but he who shuts his eyes will have many curses.

PROVERBS 28:27

3. ONE WHO DOES NOT SHARE WITH THE POOR DOES NOT KNOW THE LORD INTIMATELY.

He pled the cause of the afflicted and the needy; then it was well. Is that not what it means to know Me, declares the Lord.

JEREMIAH 22:16

Giving to the poor has been discouraged in part because of the government's failure with the welfare programs. I believe that primarily it's the church's responsibility, not the government's, to meet the needs of the poor. The government usually treats the poor impersonally. The church has the potential to be sensitive to the dignity of the poor. We can also develop one-on-one relationships with the poor to meet their immediate physical needs. Then the church can focus on their longer-term physical and spiritual needs—lovingly training and holding accountable those who are capable of becoming self-supporting.

Please consider asking the Lord to bring one poor person into your life. I pray that you and I might be able to echo Job's statement:

I delivered the poor who cried for help, and the orphan who had no helper . . . I made the widow's heart sing for joy . . . I was eyes to the blind, and feet to the lame. I was a father to the needy, and I investigated the case which I did not know.

> *Please consider asking the Lord to bring one poor person into your life.*

GIVING TO SECULAR CHARITIES

Numerous secular charities (such as fraternal orders or organizations formed to conquer various diseases) compete vigorously for our gift dollars. Scripture does not address whether or not we should give to these charities. However, my wife and I have decided not to normally support these organizations with our gifts. Our reason is that while many people support secular charities, only those who know the Lord support the ministries of Christ. We have occasionally given to secular charities either when the solicitor was a friend we wanted to encourage or influence for Christ, or when we sensed the Lord prompting us to give.

PONDER YOUR FUTURE

As you begin a career, you will have more income to manage and will have the opportunity to give larger amounts.

I want to encourage you to purpose in your heart that from the very beginning — starting with the very first paycheck — you will be a faithful, consistent giver. The most fulfilled people I have known in my business career are those who have been generous.

There is a great temptation to put off giving with the idea in mind, *"I just graduated, I deserve . . ."*

I assure you: If you purpose in your heart to be generous from the very beginning, even if it means a short-term sacrifice, you will spend an eternity reaping the blessings for it.

Consistently Save—

"Steady plodding brings prosperity."

PROVERBS 21:5

**MEMORIZE
PROVERBS 21:20, LB**
"The wise man saves for the future, but the foolish man spends whatever he gets."

PROVERBS 21:5, LB
"Steady plodding brings prosperity; hasty speculation brings poverty."

PRACTICAL APPLICATION
Complete the Insurance and Investing practical applications.

DAY ONE _____

Read Genesis 41:34-36; Proverbs 21:20 and Proverbs 30:24-25 and answer:

What do these passages communicate to you about savings?

Genesis 41:34-36 —

Proverbs 21:20 —

Proverbs 30:24-25 —

Read Luke 12:16-21, 34.

Why did the Lord call the rich man a fool?

According to this parable, why do you think it is scripturally permissible to save only when you are also giving?

DAY TWO

Read 1 Timothy 5:8 and answer:

What is a scripturally acceptable goal for saving?

Then read 1 Timothy 6:9.

What is a scripturally unacceptable reason for saving?

Then read 1 Timothy 6:10.

According to this verse, why is it wrong to want to get rich (refer to *1 Timothy 6:9*)? Do you have the desire to get rich?

Then read 1 Timothy 6:11.

What should you do if you have the desire to get rich?

DAY THREE

Read Proverbs 21:5; Proverbs 24:27; Proverbs 27:23-24; Ecclesiastes 3:1; Ecclesiastes 11:2 and Isaiah 48:17-18.

What investment principle can you glean from each of these verses, and how will you apply each principle to your life?

Proverbs 21:5—

Proverbs 24:27—

Proverbs 27:23-24—

Ecclesiastes 3:1—

Ecclesiastes 11:2—

Isaiah 48:17-18—

DAY FOUR _____

Gambling is defined as playing games of chance for money, betting, taking great risks and speculating. Some of today's most common forms of gambling are casino wagering, betting on sporting events, horse races, gambling over the Internet and state-run lotteries.

What are some of the motivations that cause people to gamble?

Do these motives please the Lord? Why?

Read Proverbs 28:20 and Proverbs 28:22.

According to these passages, why do you think a godly person should not gamble (play lotteries, bet on sporting events, etc.)?

How does gambling contradict the scriptural principles of working diligently and being a faithful steward of the Lord's possessions?

DAY FIVE_____

Read the *Saving Notes* and answer:

What was the most important information in the notes?

How will you apply this to your life?

DAY SIX
PONDER YOUR FUTURE_____

Carefully study the principle of compounding on page 134. Assume you saved $20 each week (about $1,000 per year) and earned ten percent. How much would you accumulate by age 65 if you started this saving plan today?

$ _____ (Refer to the graph on page 135.)

Describe the specific steps you intend to take to begin saving.

My prayer request for the coming week:

INVESTING NOTES

SAVING

The first step in investing is saving. Unfortunately, most people are not consistent savers. The average person in our country is three weeks away from bankruptcy. He has a relatively expensive lifestyle, significant monthly credit obligations, little or no money saved, and he is totally dependent on next week's paycheck to keep the budget afloat.

Scripture encourages us to save. *"The wise man saves for the future, but the foolish man spends whatever he gets"* (Proverbs 21:20, LB). The ant is commended for saving for a future need. *"Four things on earth are small, yet they are extremely wise; ants are creatures of little strength, yet they store up their food in the summer"* (Proverbs 30:24-25, NIV). Savings is the opposite of debt. Saving is making **provision for** tomorrow, while debt is **presumption upon** tomorrow.

I call saving the "Joseph principle," because saving requires self-denial. Joseph saved during the seven years of plenty to survive during the seven years of famine. The essence of saving is denying an expenditure today so that you will have something to spend in the future. One of the major reasons most people are poor savers is because we live in a culture of self-indulgence, not self-denial. When we want something, we want it now!

The most effective way to save is to make yourself your number one creditor after the Lord. When you receive income, the first check you write should be for giving to the Lord and the second check for your savings. A compulsory payroll deduction can be very helpful to ensure that a portion of your income is saved regularly. Some commit income from tax refunds or bonuses to be saved. Please recognize this: If you immediately save a portion of your income each time you are paid, you will save

I'm sorry I took so long, Sir, but those teeny-weeny accounts are so hard to find!

TELLER

more. The Bible does not teach an amount or percentage to be saved. We recommend establishing a goal to save 10 percent of your income. For many this is not possible at the beginning. But begin the habit of saving, even if it's only a dollar a month.

LONG-TERM SAVINGS

Long-term savings are intended to fund long-term needs and goals, such as retirement income and inheritances. Pensions and retirement accounts fall into this permanent category. Except for extreme financial emergencies, these savings should not be used for any purpose other than the needs for which they were established. They could be called "never-to-spend savings." Spending these savings often results in tax consequences, and the savings are rarely replenished once they are spent.

SHORT-TERM SAVINGS

Short-term savings should be in a saving vehicle that is readily accessible. They may include interest-bearing accounts, mutual funds and so forth. These are designed to be used for planned future spending, for acquiring items such as a car, a wedding ring and your first home. Short-term savings should also be set aside for emergencies, an illness, loss of job, or other interruption of income. Financial experts recommend you establish the goal of saving the equivalent of three to six months of your income for this emergency fund.

SAVINGS GOALS

Before you develop your individual saving strategy, establish saving goals. Consider these three goals for saving:

1. To provide for your future family. First Timothy 5:8 reads, *"If anyone does not provide for his own, and especially for those of his household, he has denied the faith and is worse than an unbeliever."* This principle extends to providing for your needs in old age and for leaving an inheritance to any children you may have in the future.

2. To become free financially to serve the Lord. One objective for saving is to diminish our dependence upon a salary to meet our needs. We have the freedom to respond if the Lord leads us to invest more volunteer time in ministry. The more income my savings produce, the less I am dependent upon my salary. Some have saved enough to be free one day a week, and others are in a position to be full-time volunteers without the need to earn a salary.

When George Fooshee graduated from business school, he sensed the Lord wanted him to save steadily so that by age 55 he would be free to volunteer full-time serving a ministry. He and

> *The average person in our country is three weeks away from bankruptcy. He has little or no money saved, regular fixed obligations to support, a relatively high lifestyle, significant monthly credit commitments and a total dependence on next week's paycheck to keep the budget afloat.*

his wife, Marjean, consistently spent less than they earned and saved the rest.

The year Mr. Fooshee turned 54, he received an offer to buy his small business. The proceeds from the sale added to their savings and have allowed them to serve with Crown Ministries full time. The Lord has used George and Marjean to impact literally thousands of lives through Crown over the past eleven years. Ask the Lord if He wants you to begin preparing yourself for the future to serve Him in a financially-free capacity.

3. To open a business. Another purpose for saving is to accumulate enough capital to open and operate a business without going into debt. The amount of capital may vary substantially depending upon the requirements of each business.

ESTABLISHING A MAXIMUM AMOUNT

When a runner breaks the tape at the finish line, rarely does he continue running. But many people who have already achieved these three investment goals continue accumulating more and more. I believe that each of us should establish a maximum amount we are going to accumulate. Once we have "finished this race" we should give away the portion of our income that we were saving. This "finish line" on accumulation protects us against the dangers of hoarding.

INVESTING

People place some of their savings in investments with the expectation of receiving an income and/or growth in value. **The purpose and intention of Crown Ministries is not to recommend any specific investments. No one is authorized to use their affiliation with Crown Ministries to promote the sale of any investments or financial services.** Our objective is simply to draw your attention to the scriptural framework for saving and investing and acquaint you with some basic investments.

> "*Steady plodding brings prosperity, hasty speculation brings poverty*" (Proverbs 21:5, LB).

STEADY PLODDING

"*Steady plodding brings prosperity, hasty speculation brings poverty*" (Proverbs 21:5, LB). The original Hebrew words for "steady plodding" picture a person filling a large barrel one handful at a time. Little by little the barrel is filled to overflowing.

The fundamental principle you need to practice to become a successful investor is to spend less than you earn. Then save and invest the difference over a long period of time.

Examine various investments. Almost all of them are well suited for "steady plodding." A home mortgage is paid off after years of making steady payments. Savings grow because of compounding interest, and a business can increase steadily in value over the years as its potential is developed.

UNDERSTANDING COMPOUND INTEREST

The fabulously wealthy Baron Rothschild was once asked if he had seen the seven wonders of the world. It is reported that he responded, "No, but I do know the advantages of the eighth wonder of the world—compound interest." Understanding how compounding works is crucial. There are three variables in compounding—the amount you save, the interest rate you earn on your savings and the length of time you save.

1. THE AMOUNT

The amount you save will be dictated by your level of income, the cost of your standard of living, how much debt you have and how faithfully you budget. When you begin your career, it is our hope that you will be able to increase the amount available for saving as you implement these biblical principles.

The amount you save can be more dependent upon your standard of living than upon income. Dr. Will Norton modeled this principle. He served ten years as a missionary in Africa during World War II and earned only $150 a month. His salary supported his wife and their four young children. By growing much of their own food and spending wisely, they were able to purchase a house upon their return home.

2. INTEREST RATE

The second variable is the rate of interest you earn on an investment. The table below demonstrates how an investment of $1,000 per year grows at various interest rates:

As you can see, the increase in the rate of return has a remarkable impact on the amount accumulated. A two percent increase almost doubles the amount over 40 years. However, be careful not to make investments that are too risky in order to achieve a high return. Usually the higher the rate, the higher the risk.

INTEREST	Year 5	Year 10	Year 20	Year 30	Year 40
6%	5,975	13,972	38,993	83,802	164,048
8%	6,336	15,645	49,423	122,346	279,781
10%	6,716	17,531	63,003	180,943	486,851
12%	7,115	19,655	80,699	270,293	859,142

Time is an element we cannot control, other than to start saving now. Answer this question: Who do you think would accumulate more by age 65? A person who started to save $1,000 a year at age 21, saved for eight years and then completely stopped? Or a person who saved $1,000 a year for 37 years who started at age 29? Both earned ten percent on their savings. Is it the person who saved a total of $8,000 or the person who saved $37,000? Study the chart below.

| | Individual A | | Individual B | |
Age	Contribution	Year-end Value	Contribution	Year-end Value
21	1,000	1,100	0	0
22	1,000	2,310	0	0
23	1,000	3,641	0	0
24	1,000	5,105	0	0
25	1,000	6,716	0	0
26	1,000	8,487	0	0
27	1,000	10,436	0	0
28	1,000	12,579	0	0
29	0	13,837	1,000	1,100
30	0	15,221	1,000	2,310
31	0	16,743	1,000	3,641
32	0	18,417	1,000	5,105
33	0	20,259	1,000	6,716
34	0	22,284	1,000	8,487
35	0	24,513	1,000	10,436
36	0	26,964	1,000	12,579
37	0	29,661	1,000	14,937
38	0	32,627	1,000	17,531
39	0	35,889	1,000	20,384
40	0	39,478	1,000	23,523
41	0	43,426	1,000	26,975
42	0	47,769	1,000	30,772
43	0	52,546	1,000	34,950
44	0	57,800	1,000	39,545
45	0	63,580	1,000	44,599
46	0	69,938	1,000	50,159
47	0	76,932	1,000	56,275
48	0	84,625	1,000	63,003
49	0	93,088	1,000	70,403
50	0	103,397	1,000	78,543
51	0	112,636	1,000	87,497
52	0	123,898	1,000	97,347
53	0	136,290	1,000	108,182
54	0	149,919	1,000	120,100
55	0	164,911	1,000	133,210
56	0	181,402	1,000	147,631
57	0	199,542	1,000	163,494
58	0	219,496	1,000	180,943
59	0	241,446	1,000	200,138
60	0	265,590	1,000	221,252
61	0	292,149	1,000	244,477
62	0	321,364	1,000	270,024
63	0	353,501	1,000	298,127
64	0	388,851	1,000	329,039
65	0	427,736	1,000	363,043

Total Investment $8,000   Total Investment $37,000
Total Amount Accumulated $427,736   Total Amount Accumulated $363,043

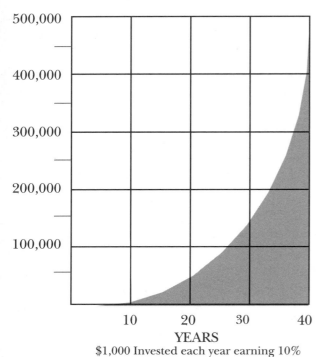

500,000

400,000

300,000

200,000

100,000

10   20   30   40
YEARS
$1,000 Invested each year earning 10%

3. TIME

Incredibly, the person who saved only $8,000 accumulated more because he started saving earlier. The moral of this illustration is this: Start saving now!

The graph to the right may help you better visualize the benefits of starting now. If a person faithfully saves $2.74 each day—$1,000 per year—and earns 10 percent on the savings, at the end of forty years the savings will grow to $486,852 and will be earning $4,057 each month in interest alone! Steady plodding pays! However, if the person waits one year before starting, then saves for thirty-nine years, he will accumulate $45,260 less. Start saving today!

SPECULATIVE INVESTMENTS

There is another serious problem I have seen everywhere— savings are put into risky investments that turn sour, and soon there is nothing left to pass on to one's son. The man who speculates is soon back to where he began—with nothing.

ECCLESIASTES 5:13-15, LB

Scripture clearly warns of avoiding risky investments, yet each year thousands of people lose money in highly speculative and sometimes fraudulent investments. How many times have you heard of people losing their life's savings on some get-rich-quick scheme?

Sadly, it seems that many Christians are particularly vulnerable to such schemes because they trust others who appear to live by the same values as they do. We have known of investment scandals in several local churches, where "wolves in sheep's clothing fleeced the flock." Below are three characteristics that will help you identify a potentially risky investment:

1. You are offered the prospect of an unusually high profit or interest rate that is "practically guaranteed."
2. The decision to invest must be made quickly. There will be no opportunity to investigate the investment or the promoter who is selling the investment. The promoter will often be doing you a "favor" by allowing you to invest.
3. Little will be said about the risks of losing money, and the investment will usually require no effort on your part. You may even be told that sometimes a portion of the profits will be "dedicated to the Lord's work."

Before participating in any investment, please be patient and prayerfully do your homework.

ED, I'M THIS CLOSE TO PERFECTING A "GET RICH QUICK" PLAN THAT I'VE BEEN WORKING ON FOR THIRTY YEARS.

DIVERSIFY

Divide your portion to seven or even to eight, for you do not know what misfortune may occur on the earth.

ECCLESIASTES 11:2

There is no guaranteed investment on this earth. Money can be lost on any investment. The government can make gold illegal. Real estate values can suffer deflation. Money can be inflated until it's valueless.

My father's friend, Mr. Russell, was very successful in the stock market. When I was a child he used to advise me, "When you grow up, invest in the stock market. It's the one sure way to become financially independent." When I was discharged from the Navy, I came home and met Mr. Russell again. The stock market was in the midst of a significant decline. He said, "Howard, I've done a great deal of research on the stock market and the *Titanic*. Do you know the only difference between the two? The *Titanic* had a band!" The perfect investment does not exist.

COUNT THE COST

With every investment there are costs: financial costs, time commitments, effort required and sometimes even emotional stress. For example, the purchase of a rental house will require time and effort to lease and maintain. If the tenant is irresponsible, you may have to try to collect rent from someone who does not want to pay—talk about emotions flaring! Before you decide on any investment, carefully consider all the costs.

> *The perfect investment does not exist. We need to diversify.*

TIMING

There is an appointed time for everything. And there is a time for every event under heaven.

ECCLESIASTES 3:1

The right investment at the wrong time is the wrong investment. The decision to either purchase or sell an investment is best made prayerfully after seeking counsel.

GAMBLING AND LOTTERIES

Government-sanctioned lotteries and gambling of all types, especially Internet gambling, are sweeping our country. A recent study discovered that **people spend 15 times more money on gambling than they donate to churches!** The average church member gives

$20 a year to foreign missions and the average person gambles $1,174 annually. Hundreds of thousands are compulsive gamblers who regularly lose their income. Many of these people are poor. One who participates in gambling or lotteries usually does so in an attempt to **get rich quick.** This is a violation of Scripture.

He who makes haste to be rich will not go unpunished .

PROVERBS 28:20

A man with an evil eye hastens after wealth, and does not know that want will come upon him.

PROVERBS 28:22

A godly person should **never** participate in gambling or lotteries.

YES FELIX, OUR PURPOSE AS THE STEWARDSHIP COMMITTEE IS TO FIND INNOVATIVE WAYS TO FUND THE CHURCH MINISTRIES, BUT WE JUST DON'T FEEL GOOD ABOUT A CHURCH LOTTERY.

© Andy Robertson

PONDER YOUR FUTURE

In the future you may marry and have children. If you do, you should attempt to leave a material inheritance to your children. *"A good man leaves an inheritance to his children's children"* (Proverbs 13:22). The inheritance should not be dispensed until the child has been thoroughly trained to be a wise steward. *"An inheritance gained hurriedly at the beginning will not be blessed in the end"* (Proverbs 20:21).

In my opinion you should make provision in your will for distributing an inheritance over several years or until the heir is mature enough to handle the responsibility of money. Select those you trust to supervise the youth until he is a capable steward.

> *Now I say, as long as the heir is a child, he does not differ at all from a slave although he is owner of everything, but he is under guardians and managers until the date set by the father.*
>
> GALATIANS 4:1-2

THE ONE GUARANTEED INVESTMENT

I was 28 years old when I stumbled upon the only fully guaranteed investment. I started attending a weekly breakfast with several young businessmen and was impressed because they were astute and energetic. But more than that, I was attracted to the quality of their lives. I did not know what asset they owned, but whatever it was, I wanted it in my portfolio.

At that time I was part owner of a successful restaurant, had married my wonderful wife, Bev, and lived in a nice home. I had everything I thought would give me happiness and a sense of accomplishment, but I had neither. Something was missing in my life.

I was surprised to hear these men speak openly of their faith in God. I grew up going to church regularly but missed hearing about a personal, intimate relationship with Jesus Christ.

A friend described how I could enter into this relationship with the Lord. He taught me five biblical truths that I had never understood before.

1. God loves you and wants you to know Him and experience a meaningful life. God desires an intimate relationship with each of us. My friend directed my attention to two passages:

> *For God so loved the world, that He gave His only begotten Son, that whoever believes in Him should not perish, but have eternal life.*
>
> JOHN 3:16

> *I [Jesus] came that they might have life, and might have it abundantly.*
>
> JOHN 10:10

When my son Matthew was in the first grade, he developed a burning desire to win the 100-yard dash at his school's field day. That was all we heard about for two months. But there was a problem—his classmate Bobby Dike was faster.

Field day finally arrived. They ran the 50-yard dash first, and Bobby beat Matthew badly. I will never forget when Matthew came up to me with tears in his eyes, pleading, "Daddy, please

> "*I [Jesus] came that they might have life, and might have it abundantly.*" (John 10:10)

pray for me in the 100-yard dash. I've just got to win." My heart sank as I nodded.

With the sound of the gun, Matthew got off to a quick start. Halfway through the race he pulled away from the rest of his classmates and won. I lost control of myself! I was jumping and shouting! I had never before experienced such exhilaration. And then it occurred to me: how much I loved *my* son. And although I love other people, I do not love them enough to give my son to die for them. But that is how much God the Father loved you. He gave *His* only Son, Jesus Christ, to die for you.

2. Unfortunately, we are separated from God. God is holy—which means God is perfect—and He cannot have a relationship with anyone who is not also perfect. My friend asked if I had ever sinned, ever done anything that would disqualify me from being perfect. "Many times," I admitted. He explained that every person has sinned, and the consequence of sin is separation from God.

> *For all have sinned and fall short of the glory of God.*
>
> ROMANS 3:23

> *Your sins have cut you off from God.*
>
> ISAIAH 59:2, LB

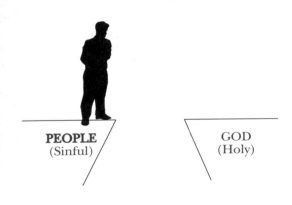

PEOPLE
(Sinful)

GOD
(Holy)

The first diagram on the left illustrates our separation from God. An enormous gap separates people from God. Individuals try without success to bridge this gap through their own efforts, such as philosophy, religion or living a good, moral life.

3. God's only provision to bridge this gap is Jesus Christ. Jesus Christ died on the cross to pay the penalty for our sin and bridge the gap from people to God.

> *Jesus said to him, "I am the way, and the truth, and the life; no one comes to the Father, but through Me."*
>
> JOHN 14:6

> *But God demonstrates His own love towards us, in that while we were yet sinners, Christ died for us.*
>
> ROMANS 5:8

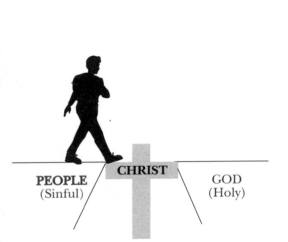

PEOPLE
(Sinful)

CHRIST

GOD
(Holy)

The second diagram on the left illustrates our union with God through Jesus Christ.

4. This relationship is a gift from God. My friend explained that by an act of faith I could receive the free gift of a relationship with God. The transaction appeared totally inequitable. I had learned in business that any time you had two people who were convinced they were getting more than they were giving up, you had a transaction. But now I was being offered a relationship with God, and it was a free gift!

For by grace you have been saved through faith; and that not of yourselves, it is the gift of God; not as a result of works, that no one should boast.

E P H E S I A N S   2 : 8 - 9

5. We must each receive Jesus Christ individually. I had only to turn away from (repent of) my sins and ask Jesus Christ to come into my life as Savior and Lord. And I did it. As my business associates will tell you, I am a very practical person. If something does not work, I discard it quickly. I can tell you from twenty years' experience that a relationship with the living God is available to you through Jesus Christ. Nothing I know of compares with the privilege of knowing Christ personally.

If you desire to know the Lord and are not certain whether you have this relationship, I encourage you to receive Christ right now. Pray a prayer similar to this suggested one:

Father God, I need You. I invite Jesus to come into my life as my Savior and Lord and make me the person You want me to be. Thank You for forgiving my sins and giving me the gift of eternal life. Amen.

You might fulfill each of the principles to become a faithful steward, but without a relationship with Christ, your efforts will be in vain. If you ask Christ into your life, please tell your teacher so he or she will be able to assist you in your spiritual growth.

10 YOUR FUTURE HOMEWORK

Learn to Be Content

"For I have learned to be content in whatever circumstances I am. I know how to get along with humble means, and I also know how to live in prosperity."

PHILIPPIANS 4:11-12

MEMORIZE
PHILIPPIANS 4:11-13
"For I have learned to be content in whatever circumstances I am. I know how to get along with humble means, and I also know how to live in prosperity; in any and every circumstance I have learned the secret of being filled and going hungry, both of having abundance and suffering need. I can do all things through Him who strengthens me."

PRACTICAL
APPLICATION
Complete the Checking Account and Budget Summary practical applications.

DAY ONE

When you begin your career, you will be faced with paying a variety of taxes.

Read Matthew 22:17-21 and Romans 13:1-7 and answer:

Does the Lord require us to pay taxes to the government? Why?

Do you think it is biblically permissible to reduce your taxes by using legal tax deductions or shelters? Why?

DAY TWO

If you marry, you may become a parent.

Read Deuteronomy 6:6-7; Deuteronomy 11:18-19; Proverbs 22:6 and Ephesians 6:4.

According to these passages, who is responsible for teaching children how to handle money from a biblical perspective?

Stop and reflect for a few minutes. Describe how well you were prepared to manage money when you left home to attend college.

DAY THREE _____

Read Luke 3:14; Philippians 4:11-13; 1 Timothy 6:6-8 and Hebrews 13:5-6.

What do each of these passages communicate to you about contentment?

Luke 3:14 —

Philippians 4:11-13 —

1 Timothy 6:6-8 —

Hebrews 13:5-6 —

In our culture today why is it so difficult to be content?

How do you propose to practice contentment?

DAY FOUR

Read Hebrews 11:24-26.

What does this passage tell you about making choices with an eternal perspective?

How will this impact you?

Then read Mark 8:36-37; Acts 4:32-37; 2 Corinthians 8:13-15 and 1 Thessalonians 4:11-12.

What do these passages communicate to you about lifestyle?

Mark 8:36-37—

Acts 4:32-37—

2 Corinthians 8:13-15—

1 Thessalonians 4:11-12—

List three lifestyle changes you have made since beginning the study.

DAY FIVE_____

Read the *Your Future Notes* and answer:

What in the notes proved especially challenging or helpful?

What has been the most beneficial part of the study for you? Why?

Reflect on your time during the study. Describe several insights you have gained from others in your class that proved especially helpful or encouraging.

DAY SIX
PONDER YOUR FUTURE_____

What will you commit to implement from the study during the next month?

What will you commit to implement from the study during the next three months?

Who will hold you accountable for accomplishing these commitments?

My prayer long-term request:

YOUR FUTURE NOTES

In this final chapter we will address several issues you will probably face soon after you leave college to begin your career.

TAXES

What is the biblical perspective on paying taxes? That's the same question that was asked of Jesus.

> *Is it lawful for us to pay taxes to Caesar or not? . . .*
> *[Jesus] said to them, "Show Me a denarius [Roman*
> *coin]. Whose likeness and inscription does it have?"*
> *And they said, "Caesar's." And He said to them, "Then*
> *render to Caesar the things that are Caesar's."*
>
> LUKE 20:22-25

If you haven't discovered this already, you may be in for a shock when you get your first paycheck. Withholding and taxes takes out a significant hunk. Many will urge you to avoid paying taxes at **any** cost. They usually rationalize by saying, "Why not? After all, the government squanders much of our money paid as taxes."

It is permissible to reduce your taxes by using legal tax deductions. But be careful! There is often a very fine line between tax avoidance and tax evasion when faced with the temptation to misrepresent deductible expenses or to not report taxable income.

An estimated $100 billion a year in taxes is lost through tax evasion. I am not condoning the waste found in government. I believe a citizen should make an effort to influence government to be more efficient. But the Bible tells us of an additional responsibility—to pay your taxes.

"Oh great, now I have to give unto Caesar, too."

It is permissible to reduce your taxes by using legal tax deductions. But be careful! There is often a very fine line between tax avoidance and tax evasion.

Let every person be in subjection to the governing authorities. For there is no authority except from God, and those which exist are established by Go . . . because of this you also pay taxes, for rulers are servants of God, devoting themselves to this very thing. Render to all what is due them: tax to whom tax is due.

ROMANS 13:1,6-7

CONTENTMENT

The apostle Paul issues this challenging statement in 1 Timothy 6:8: *"And if we have food and covering, with these we shall be content."* Study this passage carefully. It declares that if you have food and covering (clothes and shelter), you should be content. If this verse were to be restated according to the values of our culture, it would read something like this: "If you can afford the finest food to eat, wear the latest fashions, drive the newest sports car and live in a beautiful home, then you can be happy."

Our culture has been described as a materialistic, consumption-oriented society that operates on the two assumptions: (1) that more is always better, and (2) that happiness is based on the acquiring of possessions.

The word "contentment" is mentioned seven times in Scripture, and six times it has to do with money. Paul wrote,

The word "contentment" is mentioned seven times in Scripture, and six times it has to do with money.

Biblical contentment is not to be equated with laziness, complacency, or apathy.

I have learned to be content in whatever circumstances I am. I know how to get along with humble means, and I also know how to live in prosperity; in any and every circumstance I have learned the secret of being filled and going hungry, both of having abundance and suffering need. I can do all things through Him who strengthens me.

PHILIPPIANS 4:11-13

Review this passage. Paul *"learned"* to be content. We are not born content; rather, we learn contentment. There are three elements to the secret of contentment: (1) knowing what God requires of a steward, that is, how to handle all the possessions that have been entrusted to you, (2) fulfilling those requirements faithfully and (3) trusting God to do His part.

Note carefully that it is not just knowing these things that brings contentment; it is doing them. As Francis Schaeffer said, "These two words, *know* and *do*, occur throughout Scripture and always in that order. We cannot do until we know, but we can know without doing. The house built on the rock is the house of the man who knows and does. The house built on the sand is the house of the man who knows but does not do."

Once we have been faithful in the doing, we can be content

in knowing that our loving heavenly Father will entrust the precise quantity of possessions He knows will be best for us at any particular time—whether much or little.

Biblical contentment is not to be equated with laziness, complacency or apathy. Because we serve the living and dynamic God, Christians should always be improving. Contentment does not exclude properly motivated ambition. We have already discovered that God wants us to work hard. And I believe that we should have a burning desire to be increasingly faithful stewards of the talents and possessions He has entrusted to us. Biblical contentment is an inner peace that accepts what God has chosen for our present vocation, station in life and financial situation. Hebrews 13:5 emphasizes this:

> *"Let your way of life be free from the love of money, being content with what you have; for He Himself has said, 'I will never desert you, nor will I ever forsake you.'"*

> *O*ur Father knows us better than we know ourselves. In His infinite wisdom He knows exactly how much He can entrust to us at any time without it harming our relationship with Him.

LIFESTYLE

The Bible does not prescribe one standard of living for everyone. In Scripture godly people are represented in all walks of life. The Lord still places His people strategically in every level of society—rich and poor. We encourage you to consider your future standard of living. To help your thinking, let's examine several scriptural principles that should influence your lifestyle.

1. Recognize and nurture an eternal perspective. How you live and spend your money will have eternal consequences for you and others. We can either live with a view toward eternity or live focused on this present world.

2. If we waste possessions, the Lord will remove us as stewards.

> *There was a certain rich man who had a steward, and this steward was reported to him as squandering his possessions. And he called him and said to him, "What is this I hear about you? Give an account of your stewardship, for you can no longer be steward."*
>
> LUKE 16:1-2

Examine yourself. Do you spend money frivolously or waste possessions habitually?

3. Do not determine your lifestyle by comparing yourself to others. Some use comparison to justify spending more than they should. Many have suffered financially because they tried to "keep up with the Joneses" when they could not afford it. Someone once said, "You can never keep up with the Joneses.

Just about the time you have caught them, they refinance their home and go deeper in debt to buy more things!"

4. Make an effort to live more simply. Every possession requires time, attention and often money to maintain it. Too many or the wrong types of possessions can demand so much time or money that they will harm our relationship with the Lord. The quiet, simple life is the best environment for us to be able to invest enough time to nurture our relationship with the Lord. First Thessalonians 4:11-12 counsels,

> *Make it your ambition to lead a quiet life and attend to your own business and work with your hands, just as we commanded you; so that you may behave properly toward outsiders and not be in any need.*

Do not become unduly encumbered with the cares of this life.

> *Suffer hardship with me, as a good soldier of Christ Jesus. No soldier in active service entangles himself in the affairs of everyday life, so that he may please the one who enlisted him as a soldier.*
> 2 TIMOTHY 2:3-4

5. There should be an equality of needs met within the body of Christ but not necessarily equality of lifestyle.

> *For this (a gift) is not for the ease of others and for your affliction, but by way of equality at this present time your abundance being a supply for their want, that their abundance also may become a supply for your want, that there may be equality; as it is written, "He who gathered much did not have too much, and he who gathered little had no lack."*
> 2 CORINTHIANS 8:13-15

The early church was a model of sharing and contentment. This lifestyle is the perfect environment for spiritual revival.

> *And all those who had believed were together, and had all things in common; and they began selling their property and possessions, and were sharing them with all, as anyone might have need.*
> ACTS 2:44-45

And from Acts 4:32-35:

> *And the congregation of those who believed were of one heart and soul; and not one of them claimed that anything belonging to him was his own; but all things were common property*

The quiet, simple life is the best environment for us to be able to invest enough time to nurture our relationship with the Lord.

to them. And with great power the apostles were giving witness to the resurrection of the Lord Jesus, and abundant grace was upon them all. For there was not a needy person among them, for all who were owners of lands or houses would sell them and bring the proceeds of the sales, and lay them at the apostles' feet; and they would be distributed to each, as any had need.

6. A financial empire is meaningless apart from knowing Jesus Christ. Leslie Flynn in his book *Your God and Your Gold* pointed out: "Solomon, the author of Ecclesiastes, had an annual income of more than $25 million. He lived in a palace that took thirteen years to build. He owned 40,000 stalls of horses. He sat on an ivory throne overlaid with gold. He drank from gold cups. The daily menu of his household included a hundred sheep and thirty oxen in addition to fallow deer and fatted fowl."

Obviously, Solomon was in a position to evaluate whether the accumulation of money and possessions would bring true fulfillment. He did not hesitate to conclude, *"Vanity of vanities . . . all is vanity!"* (Ecclesiastes 12:8). Nothing, even roaring success, can replace the value of our relationship with the Lord. Ask yourself this question: Will you sacrifice an intimate relationship with Christ in the pursuit of wealth? *"For what does it profit a man to gain the whole world, and forfeit his soul?"* (Mark 8:36).

7. We are in a spiritual struggle. In a war you are going to use your most effective weapon. The devil's mission is to divert us from serving Christ. *"For our struggle is not against flesh and blood . . . but against the spiritual forces of wickedness in the heavenly places"* (Ephesians 6:12). In our culture Satan frequently accomplishes this by tempting us to serve money and possessions.

Serving money is often difficult to recognize because loving money is a respectable sin—people will congratulate you for acquiring the trappings of financial success. Money is the primary competitor with Christ for the lordship of our life. *"You cannot serve both God and mammon [money]"* (Matthew 6:24). Regularly examine your attitude toward money to make certain the Lord retains His proper place in your heart.

©1988 Ralph Dunigan Reprinted from the Orlando Sentinel

'My problem has been that everytime prosperity was just around the corner, so was the shopping center.'

8. Do not be conformed to this world. Romans 12:2 begins with this command, *"Do not be conformed to this world."* The Amplified Version reads this way: *"Do not be conformed to this world, this age, fashioned after and adapted to its external, superficial customs."*

We live in one of the most affluent cultures the world has

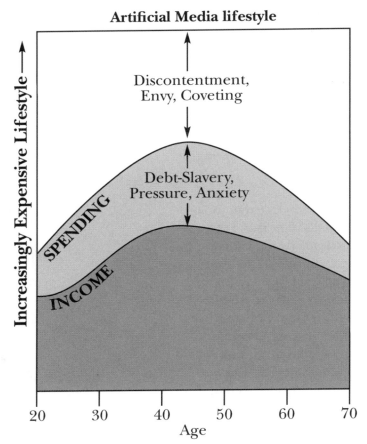

Artificial Media lifestyle

Increasingly Expensive Lifestyle →

Discontentment,
Envy, Coveting

SPENDING

Debt-Slavery,
Pressure, Anxiety

INCOME

20   30   40   50   60   70
Age

ever known. And we are constantly bombarded with costly, manipulative advertising. The purpose of advertising is to prompt us to spend money. Advertisers usually stress the importance of image rather than function. For example, automobile ads rarely focus on a car as reliable, economical transportation. Instead, an image of status or sex appeal is projected.

Reflect on the claims of TV commercials. No matter what the product—deodorants, credit cards, automobiles or anything else—the message is clear: The "fulfilling, beautiful, wrinkle-free life" can be ours if we are willing to buy it. Unfortunately, this media onslaught has influenced all of us to some extent. George Fooshee, the author of the excellent book *You Can Beat the Money Squeeze*, so aptly states, "People buy things they do not need with money they do not have to impress people they do not even like."

The graph to the left depicts how the artificial, media-generated lifestyle influences our lives. The bottom curve represents our income— what we can really afford to buy. The next curve illustrates what we actually spend. We make up the difference between our income and spending by the use of debt, which creates slavery, financial pressure and anxiety. The top of the graph demonstrates what advertisers tell us to buy. It is an image-conscious, generally expensive lifestyle that claims to satisfy the human heart's deepest needs. But if we cannot afford to live this counterfeit, media-induced dream, we suffer discontentment, envy and coveting.

POVERTY, PROSPERITY OR STEWARDSHIP?

Many Christians embrace one of two extremes with regard to finances. On the one hand some believe that if you are really spiritual, you must be poor because wealth and a close relationship with Christ cannot coexist. On the other hand, others assert that if a Christian is truly walking by faith, he will enjoy uninterrupted financial prosperity. The former assumes that godliness can only occur in an environment of poverty. Money and possessions, however, are morally neutral and can be used for good or evil. A number of godly people in Scripture were among the wealthiest people of their day.

In the Old Testament the Lord clearly extended the reward of abundance to the children of Israel when they were obedient, while the threat of poverty was one of the consequences of disobedience. Deuteronomy 30:15-16 reads,

I have set before you today life and prosperity, and death and adversity; in that I command you today to love the Lord your God, to walk in His ways and to keep His commandments . . . that you may live and multiply, and that the Lord your God may bless you.

Moreover, Psalm 35:27 reads, *"The Lord . . . delights in the prosperity of His servant."* We may pray for prosperity legitimately when our relationship with the Lord is healthy, and we have a proper biblical perspective of possessions. *"Beloved, I pray that in all respects you may prosper and be in good health, just as your soul prospers"* (3 John 2). Let me emphasize it again; the Bible does not say that a godly person must live in poverty. A godly person may have material resources.

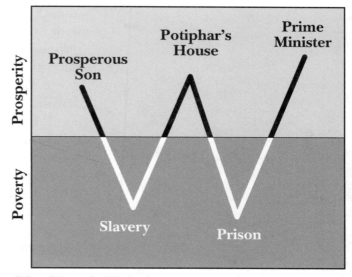

The other extreme erroneously assumes that all Christians who truly have faith will always prosper. Study the life of Joseph. He is the classic example of a faithful person who experienced prosperity and poverty. He was born into a prosperous family, then was thrown into a pit and sold into slavery by his jealous brothers. While Joseph was a slave, his master, Potiphar, promoted him to be head of his household. Later he made the righteous decision not to commit adultery with Potiphar's wife. Yet because of that decision he was thrown in jail for years. In God's timing he was ultimately elevated to the position of Prime Minister of Egypt.

The guideline for prosperity is found in Joshua 1:8. Read this slowly:

This book of the law shall not depart from your mouth, but you shall meditate on it day and night so that you may be careful to do according to all that is written in it; for then you will make your way prosperous, and then you will have success.

Two requirements for prosperity become apparent from studying this passage: (1) You must consistently meditate on the Scriptures, engraving them on your mind and heart; and (2) you are required to do all that is written in them carefully. Once you have fulfilled these obligations, you place yourself in the position to be blessed financially, but there is no absolute guarantee that the godly will always experience financial prosperity. There are at least five reasons why the godly may not prosper.

1. Scriptural principle has been violated. Look again at Joshua 1:8. There is the requirement to do according to **all**

that is written in the Bible. You may be give generously but act dishonestly. You may be honest but do not properly fulfill your work responsibilities. You may be a faithful employee but head-over-heels in debt. You may be completely out of debt but do not give.

One of the biggest benefits of this study is that we explore what the entire Bible teaches about money. Those who do not understand all the requirements often neglect critical areas of responsibility unknowingly and are confused as to why they are suffering financially.

2. Godly character is being built in you. Romans 5:3-4 reads, *"Tribulation brings about perseverance, and perseverance, proven character."* Many godly people in the Bible went through periods when they were living righteously, yet at the same time lost their possessions.

David became a national hero after slaying Goliath and was promoted to a high position under King Saul. David served blamelessly, only to be forced to leave everything and flee for his life from a tormented King Saul. Job lost his children and possessions in the space of a few moments and was described as a *"blameless and upright man, fearing God and turning away from evil"* (Job 1:8). Paul learned the secret of contentment while being held captive in chains and suffering want, even though he was righteous.

God sometimes molds our character by allowing difficult circumstances to enter our lives. For a moment I want you to think of yourself as a parent. As a father, I desire to shower my son and daughter with material possessions. But I know that if I give them too much too soon, it will destroy their character. I must wait patiently until they mature.

The classic example of how the Lord develops character in a people before prospering them is found in Deuteronomy 8:16-18:

> *In the wilderness He fed you manna which your fathers did not know, that He might humble you and that He might test you, to do good for you in the end. Otherwise, you may say in your heart, "My power and the strength of my hand made me this wealth." But you shall remember the Lord your God, for it is He who is giving you power to make wealth.*

The children of Israel had to be humbled before the Lord knew they could handle wealth.

Our Father knows us better than we know ourselves. In His infinite wisdom He knows exactly how much He can entrust to us at any time without it harming our relationship with Him.

3. The Lord disciplines His children. Hebrews 12:6,10 tells us that, *"He scourges every son whom he receives . . . for our good that we may share His holiness."* Sometimes His discipline is directed toward our possessions. You may have sin in your life or a wrong attitude

God sometimes molds our character by allowing difficult circumstances to enter our lives.

toward money that the Lord is lovingly but firmly confronting.

4. God helps us recognize our dependence. A father was carrying his two-year-old child as he waded in a lake. When they were close to shore, the child was unconcerned because of the apparent safety of the beach, even though the water was deep enough to drown him. He didn't understand his absolute dependence upon his father. However, the farther they moved away from shore, the more the child held on to the father.

Like the child, we are always completely dependent upon the Lord to provide for us. Often, however, we don't recognize our dependence when we are "close to shore" experiencing the apparent security of financial prosperity. But when our possessions are few or none, it becomes easier to recognize our need to cling to our heavenly Father. The Lord sometimes allows us to experience difficult financial times to draw us close to Himself.

5. God's sovereignty is a mystery. In Hebrews 11:1-35 we find "Faith's Hall of Fame," a list of people who triumphed miraculously by the exercise of their faith in the living God. However, in verse 36 the writer directs our attention abruptly to godly people who lived by faith, gained God's approval yet experienced poverty. The sovereign God ultimately chooses how much to entrust to each person. And sometimes we simply can't understand or explain His decisions.

	POVERTY	STEWARDSHIP	PROSPERITY
Possessions are:	Evil	A responsibility	A right
I work to:	Meet only basic needs	Serve Christ	Become rich
Godly people are:	Poor	Faithful	Wealthy
Ungodly people are:	Wealthy	Unfaithful	Poor
I give:	Because I must	Because I love God	To get
My spending is:	Without gratitude to God	Prayerful and responsible	Carefree and consumptive

Let's summarize: The Scriptures teach neither the necessity of poverty nor uninterrupted prosperity. What the Bible does teach is the responsibility of being a faithful steward. Please review the diagram above, which contrasts the three perspectives.

MARRIAGE

Marriage is one of the greatest blessings offered to us by God. A husband and wife working in unity with the Lord and with one another shine brightly as a witness to the world. Unfortunately, this great union all too often ends in divorce. Not surprisingly, the most common reason cited for divorce is financial stress. As we mentioned earlier, taking the Adult Crown Ministries Small Group Study with your fiancé or spouse can serve as a powerful vehicle to draw you together.

Young married couples often start out in significant debt due to expenses from the cost of school, engagement rings, the wedding costs and the honeymoon. The engagement ring is only a symbol of your love, and it is not necessary to purchase one that is too expensive. The wedding day is only 24 hours, but it often takes years to pay off. The honeymoon does not require an expensive, exotic location to be intimate and memorable. Excessive debt incurred in these areas will stretch your budget and stress your marriage.

STARTING OUT

A developing trend for married couples is to begin their life together by buying a home and two nice cars. The advertising media hold this up as a standard of living that they deserve. Through the use of debt, young couples attempt to live up to this "expected" lifestyle, one which likely took their parents years of work to attain. We recommend that you enter into fervent prayer and seek godly counsel prior to taking on these debt obligations early in marriage.

The challenges of two people learning to live together as one will be magnified by excessive debt. Keeping your lifestyle simple will allow for more intimate time with God and with one another. Setting aside time each year to develop goals with your spouse will help you to meet these challenges. We suggest setting long- and short-term marital, spiritual and financial goals.

CHILDREN

Parents, grandparents and teachers spend eighteen to twenty-two years preparing our youth for occupations, but generally less than a few hours teaching children the value and use of the money they will earn during their careers.

In 1904 the country of Wales experienced a remarkable revival. Thousands of people were introduced to Christ in a period of nine months, and the results were dramatic! Bars closed because of lack of business. Policemen exchanged their weapons for white gloves as crime disappeared. Horses did not understand their drivers as profanity was no longer uttered. Wales was so evangelically minded that it sent missionaries all over the world.

One of those missionaries traveled to Argentina where on the streets he led a young boy to Christ. The boy's name was Luis Palau. He has since come to be known as the "Billy Graham" of Latin America.

Out of gratitude for this Welsh missionary, Palau decided to go to Wales to express his thankfulness to that country for helping lead him to Christ. What he discovered was astonishing. Less than one-half of one percent of the Welsh attended church. Divorce was at an all-time high, and crime was increasing. Many churches had been converted to bars, and rugby had replaced Christianity as the national religion.

As a result of this experience, Palau produced a film entitled *God Has No Grandchildren*. The thrust of the film is that each generation is responsible for passing on the faith to the next. In Wales, despite tremendous spiritual vitality, in seventy years the impact of Christianity had all but disappeared.

Each generation is responsible for passing on the gospel and the truths of Scripture, including God's financial principles, to its children. Proverbs 22:6 reads,

> *Train up a child in the way he should go, even when he is old he will not depart from it.*

Parents and teachers spend eighteen to twenty-two years preparing youth for occupations, but generally less than a few hours teaching children the value and use of the money they will earn during their careers.

"IT'S A BOY, AND HE'S BEEN PREAPPROVED FOR A GOLD CARD!"

To teach biblical principles of handling money, parents should use these three methods: verbal communication, modeling and practical experience.

VERBAL COMMUNICATION
The Lord charged the Israelites,

> *And these words, which I am commanding you today, shall be on your heart; and you shall teach them diligently to your sons and shall talk of them when you sit in your house and when you walk by the way and when you lie down and when you rise up.*
>
> DEUTERONOMY 6:6-7

MODELING
Children soak up parental attitudes toward money like a blotter soaks up ink. Parents need to be models of how to handle money faithfully. Paul recognized the importance of being an example when he said, *"Be imitators of me, just as I also am of Christ"* (1 Corinthians 11:1). The Lord used both of these techniques.

He gave us His written word, the Bible, but He also sent the perfect model, Jesus Christ, to demonstrate how we should live.

Luke 6:40 is a challenging passage for parents. It reads,

"*Everyone, after he has been fully trained, will be like his teacher.*" Another way of saying this is that we can teach what we believe, but we only reproduce who we are. We must be good models.

> *We can teach what we belive, but we only reproduce who we are.*

PRACTICAL EXPERIENCES

Children then need to be given opportunities to apply what they have heard and seen. There are learning experiences which benefit the child in the area of money management and money-making.

CROWN MINISTRIES has developed *The ABC's of Handling Money* for children seven and younger, *The Secret* for children ages eight to twelve, and a study for teens. If you become a parent, you will discover these are outstanding tools to help you train your children to handle money God's way.

PUTTING IT ALL TOGETHER

You now know the biblical framework for managing money. But knowing is only half of the solution. You must act upon that knowledge. Jesus said,

> *Every one who hears these words of Mine, and acts upon them, may be compared to a wise man, who built his house upon the rock. And the rain descended, and the floods came, and the winds blew, and burst against that house; and yet it did not fall; for it had been founded upon the rock. And every one who hears these words of Mine, and does not act upon them, will be like a foolish man, who built his house upon the sand. And the rain descended, and the floods came, and the winds blew, and burst against that house; and it fell, and great was its fall.*
>
> MATTHEW 7:24-27

If you build your financial house upon the solid principles found in Scripture, your house will not fall. One of the best ways to demonstrate your love for your family and your friends is to set your financial house in order and encourage them to do so as well. God will bless your efforts.

We appreciate the effort you have invested in this course. We pray this has given you a greater appreciation for the Scriptures and nurtured your love for Jesus Christ. May the Lord richly bless you.

WHAT DO I DO NOW?

Applying the financial principles of Scripture is a journey that takes time — a lifetime. Crown Ministries has developed a number of tools to help you to continue to grow in your understanding and faithful application of God's financial principles:

1. *Your Money Counts* by author Howard Dayton is an outstanding guide to the biblical perspective of earning, spending, saving, investing and giving. It is comprehensive and easy to read. It is also available on cassette tape.

2. **When You Begin Your Career or Marriage** — We strongly encourage you to enroll in the adult version of the Crown Ministries small group study. The study will help you with the issues you will face in this stage of life.

3. **When you have children** — Crown has designed three excellent studies for children: *The ABC's of Handling Money* for children 7 and younger, *The Secret* for children ages 8-12, and a *Financial Study for Teens*.

4. **Web Site** — Visit Crown's web site at www.crown.org to learn of more practical helps, including the Crown Chronicles newsletter.

5. **Ordering Materials** — You may order Crown materials over the web, by phoning (407) 331-6000, or by writing Crown Ministries at 530 Crown Oak Centre Drive, Longwood, Florida 32750.

PRAYER LOG

"Pray for one another."

JAMES 5:16

Name _____ **Phone** _____

Address _____

_____ **E-Mail Address** _____

WEEK	PRAYER REQUEST	ANSWERS TO PRAYER
1		
2		
3		
4		
5		
6		
7		
8		
9		
10	My long term prayer request—	

Name _____   Phone _____

Address _____

_____ E-Mail Address _____

WEEK	PRAYER REQUEST	ANSWERS TO PRAYER
1		
2		
3		
4		
5		
6		
7		
8		
9		
10	My long term prayer request—	

WEEK	PRAYER REQUEST	ANSWERS TO PRAYER
Name _____ **Phone** _____		
Address _____		
_____ **E-Mail Address** _____		
1		
2		
3		
4		
5		
6		
7		
8		
9		
10	My long term prayer request—	

Name _____   Phone _____

Address _____

_____ E-Mail Address _____

WEEK	PRAYER REQUEST	ANSWERS TO PRAYER
1		
2		
3		
4		
5		
6		
7		
8		
9		
10	My long term prayer request—	

Name _____ Phone _____

Address _____

_____ E-Mail Address _____

WEEK	PRAYER REQUEST	ANSWERS TO PRAYER
1		
2		
3		
4		
5		
6		
7		
8		
9		
10	My long term prayer request—	

Name _____ Phone _____

Address _____

_____ E-Mail Address _____

WEEK	PRAYER REQUEST	ANSWERS TO PRAYER
1		
2		
3		
4		
5		
6		
7		
8		
9		
10	My long term prayer request—	

"Pray for one another." —JAMES 5:16

Name _____ Phone _____

Address _____

_____ E-Mail Address _____

WEEK	PRAYER REQUEST	ANSWERS TO PRAYER
1		
2		
3		
4		
5		
6		
7		
8		
9		
10	My long term prayer request—	

Name _____ Phone _____

Address _____

_____ E-Mail Address _____

WEEK	PRAYER REQUEST	ANSWERS TO PRAYER
1		
2		
3		
4		
5		
6		
7		
8		
9		
10	My long term prayer request—	

"Pray for one another." —JAMES 5:16

WEEK	PRAYER REQUEST	ANSWERS TO PRAYER
1		
2		
3		
4		
5		
6		
7		
8		
9		
10	My long term prayer request—	

Name _____ Phone _____

Address _____

_____ E-Mail Address _____

Name _____ Phone _____

Address _____

_____ E-Mail Address _____

WEEK	PRAYER REQUEST	ANSWERS TO PRAYER
1		
2		
3		
4		
5		
6		
7		
8		
9		
10	My long term prayer request—	

"Pray for one another." —James 5:16